Advance Praise for *Hope Always*

Everything Matthew Sleeth writes is a combination of gentle realism, biblical insight, and compassion. Given the pain and complexity swirling around suicide, a book on the topic needs all ⸱¹ ⸱ in spades. Once again, Sleeth has delivered. This is ⸱ ⸱ ⸱r those who need wisdom and hope in the ⸱⸱

MARK GALLI
FORMER EDITOR IN CHI⸱

Hope Always sounds an approp⸱ ⸱warning and yet provides ultimate hope to anyone conside⸱ng harming themselves. Dr. Matthew Sleeth's insightful, easy-to-read book is also a much-needed manual for all who attempt to counsel troubled souls battling despair. Those of us who are in Christian ministry would do well to have a dozen copies of this timely book on hand, ready to share with any who are even remotely contemplating suicide or with family members devastated by it.

BOB RUSSELL
RETIRED SENIOR PASTOR, SOUTHEAST CHRISTIAN CHURCH,
LOUISVILLE, KENTUCKY

Matthew Sleeth's mission for *Hope Always* is to save lives. He helps us understand what we can really do in our personal lives and faith communities to help people avoid "the voice of demons beckoning." These are certainly stressful times, and many are questioning themselves and the world around them. I wish I'd had this book a few years ago. It might have made the ultimate difference in helping me help someone persevere. It certainly will in the future.

BOB PERKOWITZ
PRESIDENT AND FOUNDER OF ECOAMERICA

※

Hope is the thing with feathers that
perches in the soul and sings the tune without
the words—And never stops at all.

EMILY DICKINSON

※

Hope Always

how to be a force for life in a culture of suicide

Matthew Sleeth, MD

The Tyndale nonfiction imprint

Visit Tyndale online at tyndale.com.

Visit Tyndale Momentum online at tyndalemomentum.com.

TYNDALE, Tyndale's quill logo, *Tyndale Momentum*, and the Tyndale Momentum logo are registered trademarks of Tyndale House Ministries. Tyndale Momentum is the nonfiction imprint of Tyndale House Publishers, Carol Stream, Illinois.

Hope Always: How to Be a Force for Life in a Culture of Suicide

Copyright © 2021 by Matthew Sleeth. All rights reserved.

Cover illustration of flame by Lindsey Bergsma. Copyright © Tyndale House Ministries. All rights reserved.

Author photograph taken by Corey Petrick, copyright © 2019. All rights reserved.

Designed by Lindsey Bergsma

Published in association with Don Gates of the literary agency The Gates Group; www.the-gates -group.com.

Unless otherwise indicated, all Scripture quotations are taken from the *Holy Bible*, New Living Translation, copyright © 1996, 2004, 2015 by Tyndale House Foundation. Used by permission of Tyndale House Publishers, Carol Stream, Illinois 60188. All rights reserved.

Scripture quotations marked ESV are from The ESV® Bible (The Holy Bible, English Standard Version®), copyright © 2001 by Crossway, a publishing ministry of Good News Publishers. Used by permission. All rights reserved.

Scripture quotations marked KJV are taken from the *Holy Bible*, King James Version.

Scripture quotations marked NIV are taken from the Holy Bible, *New International Version*,® *NIV.*® Copyright © 1973, 1978, 1984, 2011 by Biblica, Inc.® Used by permission. All rights reserved worldwide.

For information about special discounts for bulk purchases, please contact Tyndale House Publishers at csresponse@tyndale.com, or call 1-855-277-9400.

ISBN 978-1-4964-5001-2

Printed in the United States of America

27	26	25	24	23	22	21
7	6	5	4	3	2	

※

To you who struggle and struggled and endure

Bearing a cross upon your shoulders,

The weight known only to God;

We who love and have loved you,

Salute you,

And cry tears of thanks that God

Has given you the strength and courage to see

Another day.

Our prayer:

That you walk with God's face upon you,

Stepping out of cast shadows,

Into his light,

And that you hope,

Always and forever.

Amen and amen.

※

Contents

Introduction

Everything that is done in the world is done by hope

MARTIN LUTHER

CERTAIN OBJECTS around my house are haunted. The brass pen from my sister Naomi. The ceramic vase made by Carol that sits on my desk. The beautiful quarter-sawn oak kitchen that our cabinetmaker Josh struggled to get just right. Even the wedding portrait of Nancy and me taken forty years ago, with Mark standing by my side.

These objects have a sadness about them, but not just because the people who gave or made them are gone. At my age I've lost many friends. No, some deaths are tougher to get beyond than others. Some haunt you. It's the manner in which the people died that makes moving on so hard.

Two years ago, my sister said she was going to kill herself. She disappeared in Eastern Europe, and emails asking if she is alive go unanswered and unanswered. Last spring, shortly after installing our kitchen, Josh hanged himself. Mark, the best man in my wedding, and Carol, my childhood friend, both shot themselves.

Sad and painful stories like these are familiar to almost everyone. This

1

coming year, over a hundred thousand Americans will die by their own hand. Some will be classified as accidental overdoses, others as intentional suicides. Whether by intention or accident, for these people America was not a place of life, liberty, and the pursuit of happiness. Instead, it was a landscape of depression, addiction, loneliness, pain, frustration, and—in the end—premature death.

Suicide is a disease for which prevention is the only acceptable treatment.

What should we do? Mental health experts say we need more counselors. Doctors say we need more medicines. Teachers say we need more education. There is something to be said for each of these recommendations, but what if the men and women suffering from depression are really just the sensitive ones among us? What if they are our "canary in the coal mine"? What if we've built a world that is unlivable?

Hope Always is a guide for people who currently deal with, have dealt with, or will deal with suicide. It is for people who are struggling with suicidal ideation and the friends, family, colleagues, and church leaders who love them.

At its core, this book is both an argument for life and a plan for preventing suicide. Throughout these pages, I will offer you a perspective not typically found in books about suicide. Here we will focus on why people *did not* commit suicide rather than on why they *did*. We will also examine the limitations of statistics and dig deeply into the role of faith in preventing suicide.

If you have lost someone to suicide, my heart aches for you. And while I hope you will find comfort and answers here, this book is not primarily about easing your pain. Rather, this book is written in an attempt to keep others from hurting in the way you do now. It is about preventing suicide. Suicide is a disease for which prevention is the only acceptable treatment.

I am intensely interested in what keeps people alive. Too often, however, when looking for solutions we turn to those who have failed. When

I wrote my first book years ago, I cited the case of the two most popular books on marriage at the time. The author of the most popular book had been married five times and was the third spouse of the author of the second most popular marriage book. Although it is possible to learn from others' mistakes, we should also heed Jesus' warning about the dangers of the blind leading the blind.[1]

The beliefs and thoughts expressed in this book flow from two ancient historic streams. First, I write as a Western, scientifically trained physician in the tradition of those who have been taking an oath since the fifth century BC to "first, do no harm." Throughout my career as an ER doctor and chief of the hospital medical staff, I asked hundreds of people, "Are you thinking about harming yourself?" I committed scores of patients against their will. I pumped stomachs, intubated, and dialyzed, trying to give my patients another shot at life.

Second, my writing rests on an ardent belief in and personal relationship with the Lord Jesus Christ. Throughout the majority of my medical career as I fought to prevent suicide, I was an atheist. At age 47, I met the Lord. Fortunately, the ethics about suicide contained in the Hippocratic oath are in complete agreement with the theologies of both Judaism and Christianity. When I became a Christian, my beliefs about many things changed. However, instead of abandoning my medical beliefs about preventing suicide, I found them firmly undergirded by my new faith. They now rest on a thousands-year-old theological foundation of bedrock.

Since becoming a Christian, I have focused on a different kind of healing than I practiced as a doctor. In chapels, churches, universities, and homes across the country, I've been friend and minister to those who have heard the voice of demons beckoning them into eternal night. Homer once described their haunting song as one sung by Sirens. Have you heard it? Do you know someone who has? Although suicide is rarely addressed from the pulpit, you are far from alone. Youth leaders and elders, pastors and priests, seminary presidents and Sunday school teachers—no one is left untouched by our suicide crisis.

My faith in God is based upon firsthand experience. I am not a theologian telling you what he has read; I am a follower telling you what he has seen. I have seen at close hand what faith in the Lord can and cannot do for those struggling with suicide, addiction, and mental illness.

I am grateful beyond words to those who helped with this book. In order to write it, I met with hundreds of men, women, and youth who shared their experiences with depression and suicide. To those who communicated their stories in school classrooms, maximum security prisons, nursing homes, and churches, I thank you from the bottom of my heart.

I am especially indebted to the people who shared what got them through their dark nights and allowed them to come out on the other side, stronger in their faith and pursuit of life. Your courage and candor inspired me. Your example will save others.

This book is written in three parts. The first deals with the extent of the suicide problem we face. You can't tackle a problem until you know it exists and how bad it is. The second part examines what the Bible has to say about suicide. For the vast majority of Western history, the church and the theology of the Bible were the primary sources of wisdom on dealing with suicide. Although denigrated by many today, the church's ability to prevent suicide in the past may have actually been better than what modern medicine is capable of today. When it comes to suicide, the bottom line is the bottom line.

We who live in the age of suicide are indeed our brother's and our sister's keepers.

The third portion of the book provides strategies for applying the best of both secular and sacred paradigms to prevent suicide. I'll offer guidance primarily for two audiences: people who have a friend or family member struggling with suicidal ideation and churches that want to help. I've also included resources in the appendix that many will find helpful.

To keep this book focused and effective, we will not discuss the issue of suicide at the end of life. Although I believe the Bible does contain an ethic on this subject, the topic of euthanasia deserves its own book.

Not everything in this book will be easy to hear. Some readers will get upset with what I say and how I say it, but I believe the seriousness of this subject demands that we speak unvarnished truth. At the end of this book, just as at the end of the day, what matters is life. I'd rather somebody be mad at me and be alive.

Everything written here is designed to help you become part of the solution to our current suicide epidemic. *Hope Always* is a journey toward understanding why God sent his only Son so that we might have *life*—and have it more abundantly. I want those who are depressed among us to live. I want you to be able to help others to live. We who live in the age of suicide are indeed our brother's and our sister's keepers.

And I want the next generation to grow up in a world where pens, vases, and photographs no longer haunt anyone.

Matthew Sleeth, MD

PART 1

The Problem of Suicide

The anguish completely paralyzed me. I could no longer sleep.
I cried uncontrollably for hours. I could not be reached by consoling words
or arguments. I no longer had any interest in other people's problems.
I lost all appetite for food and could not appreciate the beauty of
music, art, or even nature. All had become darkness.

HENRI NOUWEN,
THE INNER VOICE OF LOVE

CHAPTER 1

A Tale of Two Patients

THE KEY ROLE OF FAITH IN
SUICIDE PREVENTION

❋

In my deepest wound I saw your glory,
and it astounded me.

AUGUSTINE

LET ME TELL YOU about two people I met at work. One wanted to die. The other wanted to live. They've stuck with me because of what they had in common and the ways they were completely different. I met the first on a Saturday, just before midnight. He came in by ambulance.

The patient was a man in his late twenties. He worked at the nearby naval base as a civilian. He took no medicines, had no known allergies, and had never been hospitalized. In short, he was in excellent health. He wasn't married, but a serious relationship with his girlfriend had ended three weeks before. He'd grown up locally. He had parents and an older sister living in the same town.

Thirty minutes prior to arriving at the emergency department, he made the biggest decision of his life. He did this without consulting any of the people who loved him. He placed a loaded .22-caliber pistol to his temple and pulled the trigger. A neighbor heard the shot and came running. The rescue squad brought him to my hospital.

I first met the patient when the EMTs transferred him from the ambulance gurney onto the bed at the center of our trauma room. Other than a raised area and a small entrance wound over his right temple that was covered by blood-matted hair, he almost appeared to be resting with his eyes shut. He was breathing on his own and his vital signs were nearly normal. His shirt was brown plaid, splattered with blood, and he wore jeans.

As I stood beside his bed, ordering labs and X-rays, his vital signs became less vital. I intubated him. I don't recall all the details of what happened over the next hour. There came a time, however, when if I'd been playing pinball and bumped the machine a little to the left, we would have called it a day and notified the transplant team. I pushed toward resuscitation, not for any religious reasons—I had no faith at that time—but because I subscribed to the ethic of life found in the Hippocratic oath. And so the patient was transferred, and I heard no more about him.

The next man in my tale of two patients came to the emergency department in a less dramatic fashion. The patient arrived Friday at midmorning. An ambulance brought him, but that was because he was quadriplegic and couldn't get into a car on his own. The ambulance transported him without lights or sirens. He, too, was in his late twenties. He had a fever of 102 degrees Fahrenheit. I introduced myself. He told me his name—"Hi, I'm Lee Barrett." I had to bend down right next to him to make out what he was saying. I asked him about his cough, history of urinary tract infections, and a number of other routine questions. He had difficulty forming his words. He seemed to apologize for taking my time, frequently giving me an easy and beguiling smile. He had some use of his left (nondominant) hand, none of his right hand, and none of his legs. He was unemployed.

Mr. Barrett very much wanted me to find out what was wrong and fix it. He was scheduled to spend the weekend with his parents away from the nursing home. He really didn't want to miss the time with them.

I ordered labs, a urinary analysis, and a chest X-ray and was looking at another chart when his nurse came over and spoke to me. "Matthew, do you know who the patient is in room 5?"

"Mr. Barrett?" I answered. But that was not what she was driving at. "It's the man you saw last spring who shot himself." I looked up. She nodded. "His parents are on the way. They specifically asked if you would be here when they arrive in an hour. They really want to talk with you."

Why did they want to talk with me? Were they angry? Disappointed? I wasn't sure they'd see what I had done for their son as a great favor—he would spend the rest of his life as a quadriplegic, unable to speak clearly. Although Lee Barrett had not seemed angry with me, I steeled myself for the worst.

My anxieties were soon allayed. The parents literally fell on my neck in thanks. The mother kissed me. The father kissed me. They kept repeating, "You gave us our son back!" Lee had found a reason for living, they told me. "He got his faith back!"

Got his faith back. I had heard this phrase before, but at that point in my life I don't think I'd ever personally met someone who had made this claim. With the exception of one person from medical school, I didn't have a close friend who had faith in the first place. If pressed, I think some of my friends might have acknowledged belief in an abstract creator who started up the world and was off doing whatever one does for an encore after creating a universe. But a God who could change lives? Answer prayers? Offer hope?

I was looking directly at the remarkable power of faith: faith that gives meaning where no meaning had existed before; faith that pulls the bunny of life out of the hat of death.

Yet here before me was someone who had actually made the choice to die and come as close to it as one can possibly get, and though he would never walk and might never get a job, marry, or have children, he was now glad to be alive. According to Lee Barrett and his family, his faith was what made him want to live.

Hearing about the power of faith is one thing. Seeing it firsthand is another. An emergency department is a front-row seat to the reality show of life. We get to see people from the entire spectrum: sinners and saints, commoners and kings, patients from five days to a hundred and five years old. Often we meet people at their worst. And occasionally we get to see humanity at its very best, caught in one of its shining moments.

Embodied within this family of father, mother, and quadriplegic son, I was looking directly at the remarkable power of faith: faith that gives meaning where no meaning had existed before; faith that pulls the bunny of life out of the hat of death; faith that heals the unhealable scars of life.

As an atheist, I did not understand everything that was taking place that day, but I knew as well as anyone just how much Lee Barrett had once wanted to die. Now I got to see the same man, physically diminished but spiritually healthier. I'd been concerned that the parents would be angry with me for burdening them and their son with a less-than-bright future. But that was not the case. To them, the future was ablaze with light, life, and possibilities in a way my atheism could not explain.

ATHEISM AND HOPE

What is it about faith that changes the calculus of suicide? And what is it about faith—and particularly the Christian faith—that leads to fewer suicides? We'll explore this question throughout the book. But right now, I want us to consider the reverse: How does a lack of faith influence suicidal ideation? In what ways does a lack of faith create a world that, as I suggested in the introduction, has become unlivable?

Having lived a majority of my life as an atheist, I'm well versed in what people without faith do and don't believe. For instance, a core belief of atheism is the acceptance that the universe, our planet, and all the life on it came into being by accident. If there is no God, then no God and no plan was ever involved in the creation of anything. The end point of this philosophy is that you and I are the result of a fantastic series of accidents. In short, we are all a cosmic mistake.

This dictum is at the very core of what is taught in modern secular public education. Thus, even without realizing it, the philosophy of atheism and its underlying tenets make their way into most people's thoughts. From kindergarten through medical school, my secular education taught me that life is common and inevitable. Leave the raw ingredients of the universe lying around long enough and a Shakespeare, Bach, or Newton will inevitably pop out of the primordial ooze.

Add to "you are an accident" the belief that nothing exists after death, and it becomes difficult to make a rational argument to keep going when facing a hard time. "Why am I here?" doesn't have a compelling answer without God.

It is not just individuals who come up short when they ask what the meaning of life is; society does too. If everything that exists is just the result of a series of random events, then what is the significance of humanity? For that matter, what is the significance of anything? It doesn't take an advanced degree in psychiatry to understand how "we have no ultimate reason for being" fails to bolster the human spirit.

When I subscribed to the "you are an accident" philosophy, I tended to look for meaning outside the scale of human existence. I was not alone. I read books and listened to people who spoke of both inestimably small and immensely large phenomena. I took inordinate interest in particles so small that the mere act of looking at them scatters them like poppy seeds in a tornado. When leaders of the quest to find the meaning of life in the very small found what they thought was the ultimately irreducible building block of the universe, they unabashedly, if not ironically, dubbed it the "God particle."

If the infinitesimally small fails to satisfy, one can always switch to the scale of billions and billions. From this macro perspective, we live on a planet that is a mere pale blue dot orbiting an average star roughly two-thirds of the way along a spiral arm of a galaxy. Our galaxy has a quarter of a trillion stars, indistinguishable from the 100 billion other galaxies in the universe that stretch some 100 billion light-years from end to end. In fact, if we walked at five miles an hour, twenty-four hours a day, seven days a week, it would take 575,856,000 years to arrive at the nearest star outside our solar system.

But how does comparing humanity to the tiny scale of angstroms and the immense scale of light-years help us through the dark nights of the soul? The end result of dwelling in the realm of the microscopically small and the incomprehensibly large has been dehumanization.

I recently listened to a PBS show about traveling to Mars. Thus far, unmanned missions to Mars have failed to find life. Manned missions, the scientists on the show believed, would be more successful at locating life on the Red Planet. One of the show's experts estimated that a manned mission to Mars would cost a half trillion dollars, give or take a half trillion. And what kind of life could we expect to find? A new species of orchids? Little green men? Not quite. Nobel Prizes will be given out like candy at a Shriners' parade if we discover something like the mold that grows in the dark corners of your bathroom. Many atheists believe that the discovery of life beyond Earth will put to rest the notion that God is the creator of life. "See?" they will say. "No need for God. Life just randomly happens."

IN THE BEGINNING

By contrast, the Christian faith offers a very different perspective on humanity. The Bible is not intended to be used as a science textbook, but it nonetheless offers us some clear direction on cosmology. One example is found in the New Testament book of Hebrews: "By faith we understand that the entire universe was formed at God's command, that what we now see did not come from anything that can be seen" (11:3).

In other words, the Bible tells us that once there was no universe, and then God spoke the cosmos (the Greek word often used for the universe in the Bible) into existence using nothing that existed before.

Science didn't agree with the Bible in this area until roughly a century ago. Before that time, scientists insisted that matter could not be created or destroyed and that everything that is seen had always existed. Finally, after thousands of years, the Bible and science are in agreement about the universe being formed out of nothing.

However, there's still a profound difference between the biblical and scientific view of how we got here. In the biblical worldview, behind every star, every starfish, and every stargazer is an omnipotent God who creates according to a plan. You and I are not the result of a meaningless cosmic accident. We are the result of a divine design.

The Bible includes two accounts of Creation. The first Creation account begins at Genesis 1:1 and continues to Genesis 2:3. This seven-day account generally follows the developmental pattern of life on Earth that any modern evolutionist would accept. It is told in the measured tone of a song or poem, with the repeated refrain, "And God saw that it was good."

The first account is linked to the second Creation account with this sentence: "These are the generations of the heavens and the earth when they were created, in the day that the LORD God made the earth and heavens" (Genesis 2:4, ESV).

Up to this point, God has spoken everything into existence—in seven days, generations, or an instant. This ambiguity reminds me of the zigzag architects put on a straight line when they wish to signal that the line continues, but *NTS*, or "not to scale."

Indeed, the second Creation account switches scale and perspective: God makes Adam and Eve with his own hands and in his own image. He blows the breath of life into Adam's nostrils. The implication is clear. Adam and Eve are special, outside the timeline and the normal course of the rest of creation. Humanity is the work of God's own hands. If you think that life on Earth took four billion years or so to get where it is now, the Bible gives you room to hold this view. If you believe it took seven days, the Bible gives you a solid place to stand. What it does not yield to either camp is that we are a cosmic accident.

When this biblical worldview soaked into my mind during my late forties, it transformed my outlook from hopelessness to a life of meaning and purpose. We'll get to the specifics of how the Christian faith can help us to be a force for life in a culture of suicide in part 3 of this book. But for now, one of the first and most important things parents can do is to tell their children they are not an accident. Children should be told that they are an intentional creation of God. Their purpose is to discover the plan that God has for their life. In doing so, they will "glorify God and enjoy him forever."

One of the most important things parents can do is to tell their children they are not an accident.

I suspect that many reading this book did not hear that message as a child. I didn't. In fact, on a number of occasions, my mother told us kids that she wished she'd never had us. Her life wasn't easy, and I don't think she meant to harm her children through what she said, but that was the message we received.

Yet despite her communications and a pervasive secular message that I had no ultimate purpose, I always felt that I was here for a reason. As an atheist, where did this belief come from?

The notion that I was here for a purpose was implanted in my brain when I was five. I remember when it happened. My 103-year-old great-aunt took me by my shoulders, looked me straight in the eye, and said, "God has a plan for you, Matthew. He knows how much mischief you can get into. That's why he's given you two angels." And then she glanced over each of my shoulders as if she could actually see my guardians.

To this day, I believe that my great-aunt meant what she said. Recalling her words over half a century later still brings me great comfort and joy. She wasn't saying I was a good little boy or telling me I could be anything I wanted to be when I grew up. She was doing something far more important: she was giving me a philosophy of life, the philosophy of purpose. She was nourishing my soul.

Proverbs 15:4 tells us that kind words are a tree of life. My great-aunt planted a seedling in my soul that day that has been sorely tested—through seasons of drought and disease, troubles and turmoil—but has never died. As a Christian, I am now convinced it will never die.

My aunt could have taught me how I was made up of 37 trillion cells, each of which was made of 100 trillion atoms, which were in turn composed of countless protons, neutrons, and electrons, which in turn were made up of . . . and so on. That knowledge, though true, would not have nourished me as much as telling me I was made by God for a purpose. In short, my great-aunt was the first to tell me clearly and definitively: you are not an accident!

Whether you are a man or a woman, you are made in God's image. You are not an accident or a mistake. You are exactly what God intended you to be. Moreover, you don't have to choose between science and God, fact and faith. God invented science, and science is just catching up to God.[1]

You may read the opening chapters of Genesis to mean seven twenty-four-hour days, an instant, or billions of years, but that does not impact why you are here. What must be taken literally is that we are the intentional masterpieces of an omnipotent God—made in his image. We are not mistakes in a vast, seemingly meaningless universe.

Science fiction movies and conjecture to the contrary, life is rare. Intelligent life that writes symphonies and splits atoms is rarer still. Other life may be found on other planets, but so far as anyone knows for a fact, you and all the life on Earth are extraordinary and may be unique. Any statement to the contrary is either pure conjecture or an outright lie. The Bible called the manner in which the universe came into existence several thousand years before science did. I'll go with it. You should too. Sit back and let the idea that you were made by God for a purpose seep into your mind.

SEARCHING FOR MEANING APART FROM GOD

As we've seen, our search for meaning—and where we look for it—has a great impact on our view of life. As an atheist, I subscribed to a philosophy that tried to find meaning in science. But science is just one of the many places we look to find meaning apart from God. An even more popular way is the pursuit of money and possessions.

There is a billboard on the highway near where I live that features a woman holding a shopping bag. "Happy" is the caption over her head. On the same billboard is another picture of the same woman sporting a bigger smile. She is holding three shopping bags. "Happier" is the caption over her head. It's not an ad for a clothing company or the maker of fancy shopping bags. The ad is for a bank. The message is that this bank's credit card can help you get more things, and that this will result in you being happy . . . or, rather, happier.

Go ask financial planners (I did), and you will find that their clients who have $100,000 invested believe they will be happier when they have saved $200,000. Those with $200,000 believe they will be happier when they reach $400,000. Remarkably, the planners say the belief that more money leads to more happiness is not linear. By the time folks have one million saved, they long for the day when they will have three million. Does more money equal more happiness?

Having grown up at and below the poverty level, I know something of economic uncertainty. I was living on my own by the time I was sixteen. It was not always easy. I've been so hungry that I've eaten out of a dumpster. I've also had the income of a physician. In my experience, a certain level of income and economic stability is a blessing.

This past winter, I hit a moon-sized crater in the road. Instantly my tire went flat. It was sleeting and cold. Even so, I literally bowed my head and thanked the Lord. It is a blessing to be in a place where one blown tire does not result in economic disaster—as it would have earlier in my life and as it might for so many others today. However, past a fairly modest income, every study undertaken has shown diminishing returns when it comes to happiness and increasing income.

If more money equaled more happiness, then as one of the richest countries on earth (and in history), the United States would also be one of the happiest places on earth. But sadly, we are not. We are one of the most anxious and depressed societies. Still, the dictum that more money equates to more happiness is one of the most pervasive beliefs in our society. Why?

Some people just like having more and more money even if they have no intention of spending it. These people are known as misers. But for most, more money represents more buying power—like the person pictured on the billboard. More money equals more things. And oh, how many things there are.

In 1970, the average American saw five hundred advertisements a day. Today, we view five thousand. Eight companies alone spent $28 billion on advertising last year. In 2018, all companies spent an estimated $151 billion on advertising, or $462 for every man, woman, and child in the country.[2] What is being advertised? Everything! Electronics, fast food, beauty products, television, movies, music, coffee, alcohol, clothing—on and on it goes.

Almost everything that we see in ads is sold using one promise. Advertisers for these products and services may say that they will make us more secure, better looking, more popular, and so on, but underneath each of these promises lies the great brass ring. Whether it is a car, a computer, or a cruise to a foreign land, each and every purveyor of a product explicitly or implicitly promises to make us happier *if* we buy their product. Indeed, would anyone buy something if it promised to make us unhappy?

In order to appeal to our longing to be happy, advertisers depict happiness even if they are selling something as mundane as a toothbrush. Models smile while they shave, apply eyeliner, wear new shoes, talk on new phones, and shop online. They smirk with self-satisfaction as they drive new cars down uncrowded city streets or purchase auto insurance from nonexistent insurance stores where animated chameleons and ostriches work.

No one, and I mean no one, grins when they buy auto insurance—even if it is bundled with their homeowner's policy. These ads are lies or, at best, distortions of the truth. They set up an unrealistic expectation that happiness

———————※———————

Perhaps happy and happier don't come in shopping bags as we've been led to believe.

———————※———————

can be obtained through buying things. The more ads we see featuring smiling models, however, the less happy our nation becomes. Perhaps happy and happier don't come in shopping bags as we've been led to believe.

FAME GAMES AND CREATURE COMFORTS

Another avenue that promises meaning is the attainment of fame. Perhaps if others like us or follow us or give us the thumbs up, we will have found purpose for our lives. The advent of social media makes this pursuit accessible to all. But judging from the number of celebrities and people at the top of their fields who have committed suicide, fame is not all that it is advertised to be either.

Still another path to meaning is comfort—catering to our physical desires. With enough comfort, we think, we can finally be content. We search for comfort wherever it can be found—in luxuries, in sex, and in food.

I was in a hotel room recently and turned on the television. A reality show was airing about people who weigh more than a quarter of a ton. My heart couldn't help but go out to these people. Once in their lives they were able to do cartwheels and hang upside down at the playground. Now they had difficulty moving from one oversized recliner to another. And what did the ads from this show feature? Fast food—with the announcers telling us that our deepest gustatory cravings could be satisfied in moments. But can the hunger we feel and the recognition we crave be satisfied by any amount of food or any number of "followers"?

WATCHING AND BEING WATCHED

Some search for meaning by trying to be unique. We live in a world that tells us that we can be anything we want to be, and sometimes this almost seems real. From the top of our head to the tips of our toes, if we don't like what we see, we can be something else. It's no longer a matter of growing your hair long if it is short or shaving it off if it is long. Curly hair can be straightened and straight hair curled. Blondes can become black haired and vice versa, and we can even color our hair like our favorite cartoon characters. Or if we're tired of living in the skin we were born in, we can visit a tattoo parlor or plastic surgeon to discuss options.

If these attempts fail to satisfy, we can always try to escape our lives through entertainment. Each year, Americans spend around eleven solid weeks watching television. We spend another five and a half solid weeks on social media sites. More than half of teens spend another five and a half weeks a year playing games on computer platforms. In total, it is estimated that teens spend 7.5 hours a day staring at screens for entertainment purposes. By the time the average American turns eighteen, they will have viewed 200,000 acts of violence in cartoons, television shows, and movies.[3] And apparently, we like to watch other people have sex. Americans watch more pornography than any other country.

Another form of entertainment is sports. We can tune into one of several hundred dedicated sports channels around the globe. Here we can watch solid, semisolid, and compressed air in balls that are hit, passed, kicked, and butted through various artificial boundaries, posts, holes, and hoops twenty-four hours a day, seven days a week. We can watch cars, horses, people, dogs, sleds, and bicycles race in lines, circles, and loops.

And if all of these fail to bring us joy, there are always drugs and alcohol, which are another means of escape.

Not all the activities, products, and beliefs mentioned above are bad in and of themselves. But all of these things—when used as an avenue to provide purpose and meaning in life—will ultimately disappoint. They fail to answer the big questions in life: Why am I here? What is my purpose? How will I find meaning and happiness? What happens to me when I die?

No matter how big or small we think, no matter how many ways we choose to distract and entertain ourselves, if our philosophy of life doesn't have answers for these questions, we will have difficulty making it through the tough times that each of us inevitably encounters.

WE ARE ALL LEE BARRETT

What makes it so that one person wants to end their life during a difficult time, while another makes it through? How does one person respond positively to adversity that another finds unbearable? How can both be true in the same person?

Let's revisit my quadriplegic patient. In the case of the Lee Barrett who wanted to die versus the Lee Barrett who wanted to live, both grew up in the same house. Both had the same mother. Both had the same father. Both had analogous educations. Both were raised in the same environment. Both had the same friends. One had health and a job—but that is not the one who wanted to live. The main difference in who wanted to live and who wanted to die was faith. It has long been known that faith plays a protective role when it comes to suicide. Those who believe in God are between four and six times less likely to commit suicide as those who don't.[4]

Why? Does faith make people happier? Are believers more fearful of the consequences of suicide? Are they more likely to take into account the pain they will cause others? Do they find solace in having a God in charge of their lives?

The Christian faith I espouse in this book is not a cure-all. Even as Jesus walked the roads of ancient Israel, he did not cure every leper. As our secular culture forms us, the futile places we search for meaning, like the ones I described in this chapter, affect both those in the church and those without. And as the current rate of suicide increases in our overall population, it will increase in Christians as well—but at a reduced rate from the general population. Indeed, Christianity's protective effect in preventing suicide has been established through multiple studies over the last century. To my knowledge, no exceptions to these findings have been found.

Yet it is also a fact that all of us—those with faith and those without—will face tough times in this life. The Bible and experience confirm that it is not a matter of *if* we experience grief and sorrow; it is *when*. Our health will decline. Our looks will fade. Everyone we love will die. All of the possessions we worked so hard for will eventually turn to dust. Try as we might, we can take nothing with us to the grave.

From a biblical worldview, we are all Lee Barrett. We all have moments when we wish we were dead. And we all face situations when we would give anything to have another minute with a loved one.

In the next chapter, we will examine the depth, extent, and urgency of our suicide crisis and begin laying a foundation for a path forward.

CHAPTER 2

The Greatest Depression

THE SUICIDE CRISIS IS MUCH, MUCH
WORSE THAN WE EVER IMAGINED

※

Darkness is my closest friend.

PSALM 88:18

IN THE COMING YEAR, ten million Americans will ponder ending their life. It is almost a certainty that someone you love has thought, is thinking, or will think about suicide. What will you say to them? How will you deal with suicidal thoughts if they cross your own mind?

People are hearing and seeing a lot about suicide too. They read online and in papers about children, neighbors, and celebrities who have taken their own lives. They see suicides in musicals, movies, and television shows. They read about suicides in books. They hear about suicide in songs.

People are not just seeing, hearing, and thinking about suicide; they are killing themselves in droves. More than five Americans will intentionally kill themselves in the coming hour. The body count adds up quickly: 130 people per day; 3,900 per month; 47,000 per year; nearly half a million in the coming decade.*

---

*Numbers and statistics can help us understand things. But not everyone enjoys them. My wife had math anxiety dreams for decades even after she was a college English professor. Further, many reading this book are aware through personal experience that suicide is a major problem. If you belong to either of these camps and you wish to go straight to the portion of this book that deals with making things better, you have not only my permission but my blessing to skip the rest of this chapter (and even the remainder of part 1) and forge ahead. However, if you wish to know just how bad the suicide phenomenon is, read on.

More than five Americans will intentionally kill themselves in the coming hour.

Not since the Great Depression has the suicide rate been so high. How high is high, and how exactly does the current suicide rate compare with that seen during the Great Depression? In 1930 there were 123 million people living in America. Today, we number one-third of a billion.

In order to compare one time period to another, statisticians count suicides, marriages, divorces, and births by their occurrence per one thousand, one hundred thousand, or one million people. This in theory allows an apples-to-apples comparison. When we do this with suicides, we find that the suicide rate today has reached that seen during the Great Depression: approximately 14 suicides per year per 100,000 people.[1]

But as we'll see, the problem is much worse than it first appears.

APPLES TO APPLES?

At first blush, the suicide rate today appears to be the same as that seen in the Great Depression. The suicide rate during the 1930s alarmed the nation then, just as many are alarmed today.

Statistics are useful things. They can wake us up to ominous trends. But they also have their limitations. Various factors can cause errors and differences in how we interpret and handle statistics. Are we looking at studies produced by the government, medical specialty boards, the Centers for Disease Control and Prevention, or the World Health Organization? Have we taken into account over- or underreporting, biases, and other potential flaws in a study's design?

Still, even accounting for such factors, a suicide rate of 14 per 100,000 during the Great Depression and 14 per 100,000 today would appear to be the same. But this is where Internet searches, online encyclopedias, and raw statistics will leave you high and dry. Because the suicide rate then and the suicide rate today aren't in the same ballpark—they're not even in the same zip code. When we look at the numbers from the two periods, we are not comparing apples to apples, or even apples to oranges. We might as well try comparing apples to space stations.

In order to compare suicide rates, we need to back up from the narrow-angle view afforded by suicide statistics and broaden our view to that of a generalist's. From this vantage point we see clearly that a suicide rate per 100,000 gathered today has little relationship to one taken nearly a century ago. Why? Because it is a lot harder to kill yourself today than it was in 1930.

Today, we have drugs that can be used to reverse the effects of over-doses. We have medicines that can bind toxins before they do harm. We have reliable ventilators in hospitals, with staff trained to use them, which can be employed to breathe for a patient until the poison they've ingested or injected wears off. We have dialysis machines to remove other poisons from the bloodstream.

On top of all these advances, we have regional trauma and poison control centers. Our nationwide emergency medical system is accessed by a universal 911 system, which is tied to mobile rescue units manned by highly trained EMTs and paramedics. A not insignificant number of those who attempt suicide by firearms, knives, or jumping can be saved if treated within trauma's "golden hour." In 1930, most homes in America didn't have a rotary landline, let alone mobile phones that can summon help in seconds, anywhere, at any time.

Deaths attributable to suicide are the tip of the iceberg. In 2018, there were more than 48,000 suicides in the United States, *but* there were 1.4 million suicide *attempts*.[2] Without our advanced medical systems, I believe that our current suicide rate would be far greater than at any other time in history.

Only if we could transport the people who attempt suicide this year back to the 1930s for treatment would we be able to compare the current suicide epidemic to that of its previous high in our country. I saw some 30,000 patients in the emergency department during my medical career. I (optimistically) estimate that I could have saved only 10 to 20 percent of the suicide attempts we were able to rescue if I had been operating in a 1930s hospital, equipped with the typical labs, equipment, and medicines from that time. Many hospitals didn't even have emergency departments or casualty wards in the 1930s. They had no instant chemical assays to identify toxins, much less drugs like Narcan or Digibind to reverse their effects. Realistically, my save rate would probably have been even lower.

America is in the midst of the greatest depression it has ever experienced.

In other words, if we transported all the suicide attempts from this year back to the 1930s to be treated, we might see a death toll of 1.2 million. Round the numbers down by another 20 percent to be conservative, and America would currently be experiencing an annual death toll of one million a year from suicide. If the suicide rate in the Great Depression was 14 per 100,000, then today's rate (adjusted for technology) would be somewhere in the neighborhood of 300 per 100,000.

The problem we are dealing with is far worse than the already staggering death toll would indicate. America is in the midst of the greatest depression it has ever experienced.

IT GETS EVEN WORSE

In the 1930s there were no clinically proven medications to treat depression, and the suicide rate was as high as it is today. As we have just seen, our suicide rate might be closer to the 300 per 100,000 range when adjusted for technologies. But we live in the age of pharmacology. Americans are currently taking antidepressants at a higher rate than ever. Today, roughly one in eight American adults is taking a medication to treat depression, and *still* the suicide rate is up 30 percent in the last twenty years.[3] What would happen if our population lived in the 1930s, when no reliable pharmacological treatments for depression were available?

Moreover, our suicide stats today are leaving out critical data. People are killing themselves en masse, but many of these deaths are not counted as suicides. Overdoses of drugs such as alcohol, narcotics, synthetic narcotics, barbiturates, cocaine, benzodiazepines, and methamphetamines are listed as "accidental" by our current system for recording causes of death. It is reasonable to assume that at least some of these deaths are intentional or at best reveal a near-suicidal ambivalence toward life. I believe that in many instances, if someone were found dead with a heroin-filled syringe in their arm in 1930, they were counted as a suicide.

For many, the times we are living through are not characterized by happiness but a morose sense of confinement, a wish to escape life, or an outright rejection of life. In 2017, there were nearly 120,000 combined deaths due to intentional suicide and accidental overdoses. And still, the body count grows.

AND IT WILL LIKELY WORSEN

I gathered the above statistics in 2019, just prior to the eruption of the coronavirus pandemic. At the time, the New York Stock Exchange was setting record highs and unemployment was extraordinarily low. Still, the suicide rate in America had risen 30 percent in the prior twenty years. Why so much unhappiness while our economy was booming?

During the Great Depression, the Farm Security Administration sent out photographic artists like Dorothea Lange to document the country's depression. She captured the desperation of those who had lost everything. She documented the "why" of the Great Depression. Journalists wrote about the reasons. If you asked the average person then why the country was depressed, they could tell you. In the 1930s, one out of every four Americans was out of work. Waves of humanity were driven to despair by crop, stock market, and bank failures. Our country was blighted by millions of acres of foreclosed farms sinking under oceans of dust. Breadlines, soup kitchens, and work camps filled the landscape.

If a government agency had sent photographers in 2019 to document our suicidal population, where would they aim their cameras? What do you think was the cause of such widespread unhappiness? Economic depressions may be easier to capture on camera than spiritual depressions, yet both are deadly.

What would happen to us if we encountered the same hardships faced by our grandparents in the 1930s? Unfortunately, that question is no longer hypothetical. In spring 2020, millions lost jobs. Stores and restaurants failed. Death tolls rose at alarming rates. And experts in multiple fields have predicted that the pain may have only just begun. Not surprisingly, calls to suicide hotlines during the spring 2020 coronavirus lockdown were up 800 percent.[4]

In preparing to write this book, I reviewed texts ranging across centuries. One book that I was particularly struck with and read cover to cover was published twenty years ago. It's about the (then) alarming increase in suicide. The book was lauded by reviewers and on bestseller lists. The author gives the history of suicide and the current state of treatment. It is a well-written book. The author, a therapist with bipolar disorder herself, concludes by suggesting that we have more dialogue about suicide, that mental illness be destigmatized, that the language used to talk about it be more sensitive, that groups with lifestyles which had previously been marginalized and who had very high suicide rates be mainstreamed, and that access to mental health services be increased.

The author suggests that more people might benefit from the use of antidepressants and mood stabilizers, including lithium, a drug she herself had benefited from. (Lithium has consistently and singularly been shown to not only treat depression but also to lower the incidence of suicide.)

The book's conclusions are not unique. Almost every book written on the subject in the last two decades agrees with its conclusions. But here is the problem: society has followed the book's advice for the past twenty years, and things have only gotten worse.

THE FIRST STEP

It is said that the first step in correcting a problem is to recognize that there is a problem. As a country, we are in the midst of the greatest spiritual depression we have ever known. What should we do? Where, or to whom, should we turn for help?

Listen to any mental health expert today, and you will hear an impassioned cry to redouble our current efforts. I believe this sentiment is right but the conclusion is wrong. Doing more of the same thing while expecting a new result—as the saying goes—is the definition of insanity.

Admitting the problem is the first step in solving it, but we often do the complete opposite with our most intractable problems. One method of dealing with problems is to declare that they no longer exist. In other words, we say that something that was once wrong no longer is. Put this way, a suicide rate of 14 or 20 or 30 per 100,000 is only bad or wrong if we define it as wrong.

We can draw a parallel from another societal phenomenon. Once upon a time in America, divorce was rare. A mere century ago, society considered divorce to be a gross moral failure. Being divorced didn't just exclude one from things like ministry and teaching in schools; public office was off limits if a person was divorced.

Between 1900 and 1960, the divorce rate in America doubled. After no-fault divorce legislation was passed in 1967, the divorce rate doubled again in just a decade.[5] Society sounded the alarm. Books were written, hearings were held, forums convened, and a whole new industry of marriage counseling was born. Nonetheless, as more and more people divorced, came from divorced families, or had divorced friends, pressure mounted to destigmatize divorce. What had once been considered a tragedy was downgraded to one of life's annoyances. Once taboo, divorce became standard fare in movies, songs, and literature. Today, approximately 50 percent of first marriages, 67 percent of second marriages, and 73 percent of third marriages will end in divorce.[6]

Will suicide follow the path of divorce in our country? Will suicide become so commonplace that we'll see a section devoted to it in the greeting card aisle of drugstores? If I were to make a prediction, I think the answer is yes. If we continue on the current path, society will ultimately normalize suicide. Eventually, hoping to avoid causing offense, we will all agree to accept suicide as normal. We will invent new, less offensive language for suicide. People will no longer "commit suicide," and it will no longer be considered a moral wrong or acknowledged as an act that causes lasting damage to others. Instead, people will make a "life choice" to *stop*.

In the book written two decades ago that I alluded to earlier, the author downgraded suicide from an absolute wrong to a matter of personal choice. She (like most of us) viewed herself as a morally good person. Knowing that she might commit suicide in the future, she could no longer classify a patient's choice of suicide as wrong.

That raises the question: Who decides if suicide is wrong? Should society at large? Should those who are suicidal? Should it be put to a vote, as was done recently by a teenage girl who asked on social media whether she should commit suicide? Her followers voted that she should, and she killed herself.

"But surely," you might object, "the pain experienced by those left behind will prevent suicide from ever becoming commonplace." Don't bet on it. Again, if we use the parallel of divorce, the pain of loved ones is not necessarily an adequate deterrent.

---※---

Why, in the midst of so much prosperity and freedom, are we killing ourselves? The answer boils down to this: we are creating a world that is unlivable.

---※---

Not long ago, I met with the mother and father of a pastor in his late thirties who had killed himself. About a year had passed since the tragedy. The parents seemed more upset about what they thought were insensitive comments by well-wishers than they were about the suicide's impact on the wife, two young children, and congregation their son had left behind.

How does one grieve the loss of a son, daughter, or loved one? There is no right or wrong way per se. I have compassion for these parents, and in no way do I wish to judge them. Obviously, they were in great pain. In times of great loss, we are all full of complex emotions, often conflicting or contradictory. But I think their reaction illustrates the tendency to normalize or excuse what affects us directly. Without realizing it, we eventually silence any real talk about the causes or outcomes of suicide. Comforting ourselves in our own grief or assuaging our fears takes precedence over asking how we can prevent the next suicide.

WHERE DO WE GO FROM HERE?

Why, in the midst of so much prosperity and freedom, are we killing ourselves? The answer is complex, but it boils down to this: we are creating a world that is unlivable. As a result, our society is changing suicide from a moral wrong to a personal right. As this happens, the pain of those left behind after a suicide will be denied and downplayed, and we will begin to accept suicide as a universal human right.

I realize I've painted a bleak portrait in this chapter, and the reason is that the suicide problem in our country is real and urgent and requires immediate action to reverse the trend. But all is not doom and gloom; there are reasons for hope. The trick is getting past the bad times so we can recover the good. That's where the Life Continuum Scale, which I describe in the next chapter, becomes a useful tool. It will help us understand where we are and, even more important, the direction each of us must go.

CHAPTER 3

The Life Continuum Scale

CHARTING A PATH FORWARD

※

We rejoice in our sufferings, knowing that suffering
produces endurance, and endurance produces character, and
character produces hope, and hope does not put us to shame,
because God's love has been poured into our hearts through
the Holy Spirit who has been given to us.

ROMANS 5:3-5, ESV

SOME SAY that eating fried chicken is a form of suicide, while I think it is one of life's great pleasures. Others call a firefighter rushing into a burning building suicidal, but I say he is a hero. It's time we defined our terms. What *is* suicide?

For the purposes of this book, we'll define suicide as follows: the taking of one's own life, by acts of commission or omission, when saving another's life is not the goal of the act and the person is not acting to escape a certain, imminent (minutes to hours), and torturous death themselves.

Our definition of suicide includes the act of willfully rejecting life or acting in such a manner as to show gross ambivalence toward life.

Thus, while eating fried chicken or smoking cigarettes may be classified as suicidal by some, and may ultimately be harmful to one's health, they do not fit this definition of suicide.

I've given a definition of suicide because some contemporary books classify the act of a person who leaps from the top of a burning building as a suicide. Such a definition would include, for example, those who jumped off the World Trade Center who had no means of escape during the terrorist attacks on September 11, 2001. I do not consider this a suicide. Likewise, I do not classify the soldier trapped behind enemy lines as suicidal when he uses his last bullet on himself—if his understanding is that he will shortly be killed or tortured to death. I do not count these instances as suicides because if these individuals had another way out of their predicament, they would have gladly taken it. Therefore, our definition of suicide involves intent. Suicide is not a case of having no choice or of being forced to pick between impossible options.

When I read contemporary authors who classify a soldier who falls on his sword to avoid being tortured to death as suicide, I've noticed they avoid subjects like heroism and self-sacrifice. They take biblical cases such as Saul or Samson and try to build around them a theological ethic about suicide. In so doing, they demean and discount the experience of soldiers and others throughout history who have given their lives to save others.

Let's begin with the case of Saul, the first king of the Hebrew people, who was mortally wounded by his enemies on the field of battle.[1] He fell on his own sword to avoid being tortured and killed. The Bible does not condemn his action because it was not a suicide. In fact, Saul assessed the situation correctly. All of his men *were* killed.

The case of Samson is similar.[2] Samson, a prisoner of war held behind enemy lines, was in direct communication with central command (God). Samson asked God for the strength to bring down the building he and all his enemies were in. His country was actively at war with the country that held him prisoner. It was God who gave the go-ahead to destroy the facility. In Samson's case, we have proof that what he did was approved by God because Samson is memorialized in the "hall of heroes" in Hebrews 11.

On the other hand, by the definition of suicide I've laid out above, someone who knowingly ingests or injects a drug without a reasonable expectation that the drug will not kill them is suicidal, even if they do not die by their actions. Thus, the man playing Russian roulette with one round in the chamber of his pistol's cylinder is suicidal regardless of whether he lives through the game. Likewise, the person taking a narcotic or other drug without knowing whether it is safe is suicidal.

Our definition of suicide takes into account the state of mind of the person. I belabor these points because a student of the Christian ethic on suicide will quickly come upon modern treatises on the subject at odds with this book and historically orthodox Christian views. They will find authors with PhDs who state that the Bible has no injunctions against suicide. Some go so far as to assert that the Bible even condones suicide, using Saul and Samson as examples. Some even state that Jesus himself committed suicide. Nothing could be further from the truth.

> *Adam and Eve did the one thing they were told would kill them.*

As with all epidemics, it is important to know where and when the disease originated. In the book of Genesis, we are told that Adam and Eve were warned not to eat from the tree of the knowledge of good and evil. Stay away from it, God warned; it is poison, "for in the day that you eat of it you shall surely die" (Genesis 2:17, ESV). Nevertheless, Adam and Eve did the one thing they were told would kill them. Make no mistake, God warned our great-great-grandparents against suicide. It would be no different if someone today took a big drink from a jar of cyanide labeled "If you drink this, you will absolutely die." Indeed, if someone drank from a bottle of cyanide labeled "poison" and lived because an ER doctor treated them with a cyanide antidote kit, they have still committed a suicidal act.

SUICIDE IS UNIQUELY HUMAN

The concept of intent is crucial to understanding the whole Bible, and it is crucial to understanding our current suicide epidemic. The story of humanity begins with a couple ingesting a deadly poison. When a multi-millennia-old text gives the reason why humans do something that no other animal does, I for one am going to pay attention to it. The power of any theory is its predictive power. The Bible predicts that humans will do things that knowingly harm and even kill themselves. This truth begins on the first pages of Genesis.

As we discussed in chapter 1, the prevailing worldview today is that humankind arrived on this planet as the result of trillions of accidents played out over four to five billion years. The sole factor determining the worth of each creature is that each resultant life form is better equipped to survive than its predecessors. Although this paradigm might fit what is observed in the animal kingdom, it fails to explain why humans commit suicide.

When it comes to humans killing themselves by the thousands, the theory of evolution fails. Don't get me wrong. The "survival of the fittest" theory works for frogs and giraffes. But this book is not about how animals got onto the planet and managed to survive. If we are to understand the phenomenon of suicide, we must look for answers beyond those that apply to rats and spiders.

One basic tenet of this book is that humans are not merely super animals, the next step up on a four-billion-year evolutionary ladder. Suicide is unknown in the animal kingdom. It doesn't fit with any evolutionary model. Humans are the only creatures on earth that commit suicide.

Since the dawn of time, no zebra has ever gotten up in the morning and decided not to run from the lion. Secular researchers of suicide have long looked for and would dearly love to find an animal model of suicide, but they have failed. They have tried putting too many rats in a box without enough food and chained wild animals to walls to see if they would harm themselves.

The Bible tells us that suicide was present from humanity's very beginnings. And unlike the poor caged and starved animals scientists study looking for a suicide model, we humans first committed suicide in the setting of Paradise. Suicide is a uniquely human activity, and it began with Adam and Eve. It is as old as humanity.[3]

A NEW SCALE FOR ASSESSING MENTAL AND SPIRITUAL WELL-BEING

As we go further and further in this book, we'll explore theories and theology that are at odds with the secular world, that agree with secular models, or that expand on secular thinking. As the saying goes, "All truth is God's truth." We'll look for answers wherever we can find them.

In that regard, I'd like to introduce a new tool for measuring the continuum between the most and the least suicidal persons. It is a subjective scale that describes the various psychiatric states ranging from the healthy, nondepressed, nonsuicidal person to the most seriously ill. You can use this scale to begin discerning the mental and spiritual wellness of yourself and others.

Society uses subjective scales for things that cannot be objectively measured. Some things, like height, can be measured objectively. If I say someone is sixty inches tall, anyone else can measure that person with a measuring tape and determine that they are sixty inches tall. But how would we "measure" the spiciness of food? How depressed is depressed? This is where subjective or relative scales come into play. Subjective scales can be anything from two enthusiastic thumbs up for a good movie to three out of five stars for a satisfying but not memorable meal. Subjective scales can be used to measure anything from pain to consumer optimism. The thing we need to know when approaching a new scale is to establish which end of the scale is which.

On our Life Continuum Scale (LCS), -10 is the lowest score, while a zero represents what therapists and psychiatrists would classify as a "normal" person (as far as depression or suicidality are concerned), and a +10 represents the best score as defined by the actions, words, and deeds of Jesus. While we might disagree on the difference between a +5 and a +4, we will all be able to recognize the difference between a +5 and a -5.

Let's start by describing the individual "zeroed out" on the scale and then move left toward the lowest score before we move right toward the

LIFE CONTINUUM SCALE

-10	-9	-8	-7	-6	-5	-4	-3	-2	-1
Has a homicide-suicide plan with deadly means	Has an active suicide plan with deadly means and a date	Developing a suicide plan	Exhibiting risky behaviors and ambivalence toward life	Feelings of hopelessness and helplessness	Developing thoughts of suicide	Manifesting signs and symptoms of clinical depression	Avoiding activities that promote health and happiness	Beginning to withdraw	Experiencing slight melancholy and pessimism about life

highest score. A zero on the LCS represents an individual who has no thoughts of suicide or depression. They are involved in activities that promote health and long life. They abstain from risky or dangerous activities and do those things that prevent injury, such as buckling up before driving or wearing a helmet when needed. The term "moderation in all things" could be used to describe them.

As we move to the left on the LCS, the individual develops feelings of melancholy and pessimism. We see them socially withdraw and begin to avoid activities that promote health or happiness. By the time we reach -4 on the scale, the person clearly has signs and symptoms of depression. Traveling further left, they begin thinking about suicide. They display ambivalence toward life, and they are increasingly involved in activities that put themselves at risk (for example, excessive drinking, using drugs, or engaging in risky sexual practices). As we travel further left, the individual's vague thoughts about suicide solidify into a plan. Next, they become actively suicidal and have a plan with deadly means for completing suicide. Lastly, the person develops an ambivalence or disregard for other life, becoming not only suicidal but also homicidal.

The majority of those who are suicidal are not homicidal. However,

+1	+2	+3	+4	+5	+6	+7	+8	+9	+10
Beginning of concern for others	Giving money	Giving time	Sacrificially giving time and/or money	Undertaking short-term commitments for others (e.g., hospice volunteers)	Undertaking long-term commitments for others (e.g., adoptive parents)	Forgoing one's desire or health for others (e.g., organ donors)	Operating outside comfort zone for others (e.g., missionaries)	Operating in dangerous conditions for others (e.g., volunteer's in war zones)	Sacrificially giving one's life for others (i.e., dying to save another)

the Life Continuum Scale is a *continuum*. As more people shift to the left, I believe we will see more murder-suicides.[4]

In general, the goal of secular therapists is to get a person as near to zero as possible on this scale. But from a biblical worldview, the person at zero on the LCS needs improvement. As one lives a life believing in Jesus as Savior, Sanctifier, and Redeemer, one will be drawn toward the right end of the scale.

Toward the left of the scale, an individual tends to become more and more focused on self. At the far left end of the LCS, an individual is so self-focused that another's life means nothing. In contrast, as we travel from left to right, or from 0 to +10, the individual begins to think about others and to act on these concerns. They begin to give away money and will often tithe (in Christian terms, giving 10 percent or more). They begin to give their time away. (This may include an observance of a Sabbath, or Lord's Day). As they progress right, generosity of time and money reaches sacrificial levels and affects their lifestyle. They may become involved in short-term missions or volunteer at hospice.

As we go further right on the scale, lifelong sacrificial choices become the norm. Adoption becomes more and more common, especially of children who have disabilities. They may do things such as donate a kidney to a stranger. Individuals may choose to give up what are considered lifelong desires and goals, such as forgoing marriage to better serve the Lord. Finally, they may find themselves in permanent, strange surroundings because of their willingness to serve others, typified by missionaries in developing countries. Lastly, they reach Jesus' level of sacrificial love: "Greater love has no one than this, that someone lay down his life for his friends" (John 15:13, ESV). In short, as one goes to the left on the LCS, an individual tends to become more and more focused on self, and as one travels to the right on the LCS, they tend to live more sacrificially. It's best not to get bogged down in whether some specific action is a +6 or a +7, and I recognize that all of us have days where our position on the scale may fluctuate. Remember: this is a subjective scale meant to help us understand the *direction* one's life is headed.

Although I have couched the right side of the LCS in Christian terms, Jesus acknowledges people who are not Christians living on this side of the scale.[5] I have met them serving in remote and dangerous places. The end point on the right side of the scale is the willingness to put another's needs before one's own. While getting someone to this end point may not be the goal of secular mental health-care workers, it *is* the end point and goal of Christians.

WE ARE OUR BROTHER'S KEEPERS

Let's depart from our academic discussion for a moment to see what the +10 end of the LCS could look like. To do this, let's board a ship traveling from Newfoundland to Greenland. It is the evening of February 2, 1943. The world is at war. The ship, the USAT *Dorchester*, plows through the arctic waters carrying 902 men when a German U-boat fires three torpedoes. One of the torpedoes hits the *Dorchester* below the waterline, knocking out all electrical systems and lighting on the ship. Within seconds, the ship begins to sink. Scores of men are killed outright. In the dark, panic ensues.

On board the sinking transport ship are four men. They are Rev. George L. Fox (Methodist pastor), Rabbi Alexander D. Goode, Father John P. Washington (Roman Catholic priest), and Reverend Clark V. Poling (pastor in the Dutch Reformed Church).

According to the 230 survivors, the four chaplains directed the men to lifeboats and sang out instructions to calm and encourage them. Rabbi Goode stopped a petty officer who was going back to his cabin to retrieve gloves. "I have two pairs; take these," the rabbi said as he handed the petty officer the gloves off his own hands (the only pair he actually had). The four chaplains opened a locker containing life jackets and began handing them out. When the locker ran out of life jackets, without hesitating the four chaplains took off their own and handed them to four terrified men.

Private William B. Bednar found himself in the oil- and blood-soaked brine of the sea, surrounded by charred corpses. The voices of the chaplains urging calm and courage is what he credited with giving him the inspiration to struggle and live.

These heroes were commemorated and memorialized, which is how we know their story. But not all heroes are so evident. The Bible actually says that God sees those who sacrifice for others even if humanity does not.[6] Many who are living on the positive end of the LCS are unknown to us, but that doesn't make their lives or examples any less heroic.

What I'm arguing is that if the United States is going to back away from the brink of despair, then we must do something differently. We must do what we can to raise people who sacrificially love others. A society of people who think continually of themselves will eventually implode. As Jesus said, "Whoever would save his life will lose it, but whoever loses his life for my sake will find it" (Matthew 16:25, ESV).

The world needs more heroes. When someone struggles against depression and

We're more connected than we realize. All of society loses when a single individual takes his or her own life.

suicide, their struggle is often heroic. Their battle is literally life and death. The church needs to encourage the heroism of living through struggles and making decisions based upon the welfare of others.

We're more connected than we realize. All of society loses when a single individual takes his or her own life. We truly are our brother's and sister's keepers. Plays, movies, and songs glamorize suicide, and celebrity suicides add fuel to the flame. The church needs to be a clear, loving, and unrelenting voice that says, "Choose life!" Jesus is decidedly for life, and his church must surround, uphold, and walk with those who are struggling to make that choice. (We will talk about both of these things in parts 2 and 3 of this book.)

When people perish on the right side of the LCS, they give life. When they perish on the left end of the LCS, they take life. The scale is like a teeter-totter. The greater the number of people on one side, the more all of society moves in that direction.

I've discussed that the positive values on the Life Continuum Scale are influenced by the person of Jesus. And it turns out that faith plays a crucial role in the prevention of suicide.

THE PROTECTIVE ROLE OF FAITH

For well over a century it has been known by the medical community that a belief in God has a protective effect when it comes to suicide.[7] Thirty-five years ago, even though I attended one of the most secular medical schools in the nation, we too were taught that a belief in God and involvement in a church had a protective effect when it came to suicide. Innumerable studies since then have confirmed this fact. A 2018 study published in *JAMA Psychiatry* yet again confirms this. In fact, the study even showed a protective effect on children when their parents believed in God and they did not.[8]

As I have already stated, for most of my medical career, I was an atheist. Nonetheless, in the course of seeing some thirty thousand patients, I couldn't help but notice the positive role faith played in my patients' ability to cope and recover from both mental and physical illness. In fact, faith seemed to be *the* crucial factor in most of those who successfully recovered from long-term addictions.

Intellectual honesty and an unrelenting pursuit of the patient's interest demands that allopathic physicians accept efficacious treatments from wherever they arise.

A major premise of this book is that the current epidemic of suicide and depression will only get worse if the role of God, faith, and belief is not moved to the forefront of our discussion and treatment plans. Modern medicine must leave no stone unturned in its pursuit of stopping people from killing themselves by the tens of thousands. The preservation of life is our goal. Those who have any other agenda should quit the field.

The search for treatments in unlikely places is a hallmark of modern medicine. Indeed, it is a principle that helps make Western medicine so powerful. For example, if a treatment for bacterial infection can be developed from bread mold, allopathic medicine will take it. If ionizing radiation stops cancer, we'll harness it. If the extract from a flower makes the heart stronger, we will standardize it. When leeches make a skin graft take, we'll put them to use. If the neurotoxin made by clostridium bacteria can treat migraines, we'll inject it. And if passing an electrical current through a depressed brain makes it less depressed, we will use it. For allopathic medicine, nothing is sacred or off limits when it comes to treating disease. Why then should the sacred itself be off limits?

God helps when it comes to suicide. It's a fact. Yet the current sixty-one-page report published by the CDC on suicide expunges God and faith from the discussion of suicide and depression. This mirrors a portion of the mental health-care community in the United States that has opted to put something before the health and life of their patients. It is as if the CDC has forgotten that their mandate is to eradicate disease, not God.

Let me give an analogy. I don't care for dogs. I have reasons. First, a neighbor and childhood friend was attacked and disfigured by a dog. As a teen I had a paper route in a rural area and was frequently harassed by dogs. As an ER doctor I was called on to treat the aftermath of dog attacks.

My daughter was attacked by a dog when she was a child. I don't care for dogs, yet I would be committing malpractice if I did not recommend a guide dog to someone who is going blind. Likewise, I've seen the delight a service dog brings to nursing home patients. In medical school, I was taught that the definition of a professional is one who puts the needs of their patients above their own.

The protective role of faith in depression and suicide is established beyond any reasonable doubt. Yet faith is being pushed aside by some mental health-care workers and those running suicide prevention programs. I am not the first to notice this trend toward unprofessionalism. To quote a recent study published by Oxford Medicine, "The psychiatrist cannot and should not ignore or reject religion, irrespective of personal beliefs."[9]

LANGUAGE MATTERS

By this time, the reader may have noticed that I am not using the recent politically correct language concerning suicide. I've said "commit suicide," and I have referred to people under care for depression and other mental illnesses as "patients."

These language choices are intentional. I believe that language matters. Allow me to explain. Suppose that while we are driving, we encounter water on the road. The farther forward we go, the deeper the water becomes. As the water rises and the situation becomes worse, what would be the wise thing to do—push ahead or back up?

> *It is the church's and the mental health professional's job to help people to commit to life.*

The current suicide and depression epidemics are getting worse by the month and show no sign of letting up, as I argued in the previous chapter. Should we continue stubbornly driving forward? Or would it be prudent to back up? My view is that the term "committing suicide," like the term "committing malpractice," lends gravity to the life-and-death situation it describes. In the case of suicide, it is the church's and the mental health professional's job to help people to commit to life.

Likewise, the word *patient* is meant to remind us of a virtue. A person being treated for illness or an injury (the noun *patient*) is closely related to the adjective *patient*, which refers to forbearance and long-suffering. The Latin origin for both words is *pati*, which means to suffer. This language choice does two things: it reminds caregivers of the suffering that their patients are enduring, and it reminds a society used to instant gratification that the healing process takes time.

Depression is painful. But *suicide* is also painful. The ones left behind after a loved one commits suicide experience pain that is intense and long lasting. Generations are affected. It's important to comfort those who have lost friends and family to suicide, and I know that certain language choices prioritize that. But as a former ER doctor, I'm even more concerned about preventing suicides in the future. And I think clear language will help us toward that goal.

The shifting of language to obscure truth and reality is as old as humanity. A funeral is still a funeral even if it is called a life celebration. Taking one's life is still a tragedy whether it is called committing suicide, completing suicide, or making a life choice.

This is not to say that the person suffering from depression or contemplating suicide shouldn't be handled with great compassion and tenderness. Like any other person with a disease, a measure of sensitivity goes a long way. But there are times when cures, treatments, and hard facts hurt before they make us better. Surgeons can't begin to heal us unless they first cut us open. And as I've argued throughout this book, our society is facing a grim diagnosis and is in need of urgent treatment.

ASKING IS THE FIRST STEP

This chapter has focused on others—the life-giving end of the Life Continuum Scale, the effects suicide has on others, and our need to care for those who are hurting. This last point brings me to my first specific advice for those in the church who want to help others at risk of self-harm. You will not increase the risk of someone committing suicide by asking them about it. This has been proven by many studies and by the experience of mental health workers.[10]

If you think someone may be suicidal, ask. I've found that the best way to ask is, "Are you thinking about hurting yourself?" You'll be surprised at the candor folks have when you ask this question.

The LCS can help you gauge their response—the lower their score, the more urgency there is in getting help. But never be afraid to begin with a simple, direct question. Practice saying the question out loud when you are alone, if you think that will help. Asking will not cause them to commit suicide. Asking shows you care.

Having some idea what to do next means you care even more. In the next chapter we'll learn about mental disorders and how they are classified. We'll examine strengths and weaknesses in the system and what role you might play in helping someone toward the treatment they need. For now, remember these words of reassurance from Scripture: "'I know the plans I have for you,' declares the LORD, 'plans to *prosper* you and *not to harm you*, plans to give you *hope and a future.*'"[11]

CHAPTER 4

Mental Health 101

AN ESSENTIAL PRIMER FOR
EVERY CHRISTIAN

※

*We are pressed on every side by troubles, but we are
not crushed. We are perplexed, but not driven to despair.
We are hunted down, but never abandoned by God.
We get knocked down, but we are not destroyed.*

2 CORINTHIANS 4:8-9, NLT

IN THIS CHAPTER we're going to look at some of the basics of mental disorders and diagnoses. It's not a task I take lightly. To summarize an entire
branch of medicine is daunting, yet I believe an overview will be helpful.
Any Christian who wants to help with our suicide crisis should first have
some familiarity with the various types of mental maladies. Consider this
reference material: it is not necessary to read or remember every line, but
please at least skim through it so you can refer back to it when a need
arises.

There's a well-known dictum in Western medicine: first, do no harm.
So let's begin with a few caveats and warnings. Medicine is a balance of
science and art. Medicine, and in particular psychiatry, is not as simple as
looking up symptoms in a book or on the internet. An individual's history,
genetic makeup, and circumstances matter. The physician's perspective
also must be taken into account. Occasionally the generalist has a better
view, while sometimes the specialist does. Let me illustrate with a scene

from morning rounds in the emergency department at a Level I trauma center.

An ER resident presented the case of a patient with sudden swelling at the angle of the jaw. The man was in his thirties, was otherwise healthy, took no medications, had no allergies, and had never had similar symptoms. Examination showed swelling and tenderness over the right parotid gland. (This is one of the salivary glands with ducts draining into the mouth. Saliva to help swallow food gets into the mouth this way. Also, enzymes are released by the parotid gland that begin to break down carbohydrate chains.)

Diagnosis was easy. This was a case of sialadenitis—a stone was blocking the duct draining a salivary gland. If the gland were to stay blocked, the likelihood of an infection forming in the gland over time would be great. One of us old-timers questioned the resident, "Did you have him suck on a lemon?" Yes, the resident did, but this didn't result in the stone being expelled.

A discussion ensued on the use of lemons in getting stones out. The lemon sends a signal to the salivary glands to secrete saliva—big time. We had about seventy emergency doctors as well as residents in the room. Take any ten of the old-timers present, and their combined total number of patient contacts equaled one quarter to half a million. Survey a crowd like this on a common problem, and one can quickly accomplish a retrospective study with statistically significant results.

I'd probably seen twenty to thirty patients with sialadenitis myself. The survey was done. "How often does the use of lemons result in a cure?" We each raised our hands when the percentage matched our experience. The consensus among the doctors in the room was 90 percent success using lemons.

The resident said that he'd called the ENT to see the patient in followup. At that very moment, the ENT entered the room to tell the resident that he was taking the patient to the OR to fish out the stone. The ENT turned to the gathering and imparted advice. "Don't waste your time, my time, or the patient's time by having them suck on lemons," he said. "One hundred percent of the people I see have tried lemons, and they never work!"

From that specialist's perspective, lemons don't work. The problem with his perspective was that he never saw the nine out of ten patients for whom lemons *do* work.

I say all this to give patients and families an understanding that a psychiatrist's view is different from a therapist's view, which is different from a social worker's. Outpatient and inpatient perspectives vary as well.

Medicine is an art that can be greatly influenced by perspective. Which end of the funnel are you standing at: the wide end of the generalist or the narrow end of the specialist? Both are valid.

A good practitioner also must maintain a healthy sense of medicine's limitations—something I was introduced to at the beginning of my training. On the first day of classes, the dean of our medical school addressed us. "Half of what we're going to teach you over the next four years is wrong." He paused to let his words sink in and then continued, "The problem is, we don't know which half it is."

Add the art of medicine to the practice of religion, and one must proceed with twice the caution. As the saying goes, "Fools rush in where angels fear to tread."

In the past, the misapplication of Scripture to medicine has done inestimable harm. However, this must be balanced by an understanding of history and what happens when the opposite occurs and society throws off God.[1]

SCRIPTURE AND MEDICINE

Before we proceed to our primer on mental health, let us examine one case of the misapplication of Scripture to medicine. The story involves two doctors working on either side of the Atlantic Ocean. Neither was aware of the other's existence.

The date was the mid-1800s. In Boston, Oliver Wendell Holmes Sr.

noticed and was appalled by the filthy conditions that doctors operated in. The time period was one in which autopsies were an everyday part of clinical medicine. Doctors would stop an autopsy to rush out and deliver a baby. Hands, clothing, and instruments were not washed between working on dead and live bodies. The result was a high mortality rate for mothers due to infections of the uterus known as puerperal or childbed fever.

In Vienna, the physician Ignaz Semmelweis noticed a similar pattern. The Vienna General Hospital where he worked had two maternity clinics, one staffed by physicians, the other by midwives. The physicians' clinic had a maternal mortality rate of 13 percent; the midwives' clinic had a rate of 2 percent. When Semmelweis instituted the washing of hands and instruments with a chlorinated lime solution, the mortality rate fell to .8 percent on both sides. Back in the United States, Holmes instituted similar hygienic practices and got similar results.

The doctors in Austria rejected Semmelweis's ideas. Eventually, they had Semmelweis committed to a mental hospital where, tragically and ironically, he died of an infection two weeks later.

Many physicians in America also objected to Holmes's call to wash hands and instruments. But Holmes had a standing in the United States that Semmelweis did not enjoy in Europe. Still, the Pennsylvania Medical Society revoked Holmes's license to practice in that state. This was of little practical import to Holmes, as he primarily practiced in Boston, Massachusetts, and Hanover, New Hampshire, but it does indicate the depths of dissent.

The ethic embodied in the Hippocratic oath may have preceded Christianity, but in Christianity it found a kindred soul.

On what grounds did the Pennsylvania Medical Society revoke Holmes's license? Biblical grounds. "Jesus," they said, "told us we never need to wash our hands."[2] In retrospect, this was bad medicine *and* bad religion. Jesus taught that ceremonial washing of hands did nothing to cleanse the soul. The doctors who misapplied the Scripture claimed that Jesus meant that nothing on a Christian's hands could make another person ill.

When the Bible seems to conflict with science, we should wonder whether we are reading the Bible correctly. Often the Bible has the science right and the world just needs to catch up. Once upon a time, for example, people thought that the earth was flat. Such a conclusion is actually at odds with Scripture. The prophet Isaiah wrote, approximately 2,700 years ago, "God sits above the circle of the earth" (Isaiah 40:22).

Sometimes, however, the ethic of the Bible agrees with a secular priority. This is the case with medicine. The ethic embodied in the Hippocratic oath may have preceded Christianity, but in Christianity it found a kindred soul.

Jesus healed people. This was one of the key aspects of his ministry on earth. Indeed, when John the Baptist sent his disciples to find out if the man named Jesus was the same man that John had baptized—the Messiah—Jesus responded, "I've cured the blind, healed the deaf, treated lepers, made the lame to walk, and raised the dead."[3] It was as if Jesus was saying he'd opened a hospital.

In other words, it is the business of heaven to heal. Believers are supposed to pray and work to make earth the way it looks in heaven.

As a further illustration of the close ties between the Christian faith and healing, it is not an accident that the greatest part of the New Testament was written by a physician, Luke. By word count, Luke wrote 27 percent of the New Testament, Paul wrote 23 percent, and John wrote 20 percent.

As Christians, each of us has a responsibility to work for the healing of the world. In the midst of our suicide crisis, an overview of the medical approach to mental illness will help us more effectively minister to others.

WHERE DOES MENTAL ILLNESS ORIGINATE?

Humans are complex. No two, including identical twins, are exactly the same. Ask parents with multiple kids, and they will marvel at how children from the same genetic pool and raised under the same roof can turn out so differently.

The task of a newborn is to be fed, changed, and clothed, as well as to form a bond to mother, father, and other loved ones. Any number of factors on the part of parents and family members impact these tasks.

For example, Clark, our firstborn, was severely colicky. He was born right at the start of my medical residency and inherited a milk intolerance. On top of that, his first summer was the hottest on record, and we had no air-conditioning. Eighty- to ninety-hour workweeks during my first year of residency combined with a newborn who didn't sleep through the night was a recipe for disaster. It was a difficult time.

Did we make mistakes as new parents? Of course! Did this all turn out badly? No. Our son had two parents working together to make sure his needs were met. More than three decades after his birth, Clark is one of my closest friends. As a medical missionary, he serves as the only pediatrician for two million people in Africa.

Sometimes parents do the wrong thing and their kids turn out okay. Sometimes they do everything right and their kids are a mess.

I think it makes sense to question ourselves about how we raise our children and to try to learn from our mistakes, but we also have to realize that humans are complicated. How and why we turn out the way we do is still partly a mystery. Child-rearing is not conducted in a scientific laboratory. Nature and nurture play obvious and subtle roles in making all of us. Sometimes it is the trials and difficulties that result in us becoming resilient, but sometimes the opposite happens. Things that occur when we are children can lie dormant in our psyche and come back to haunt us later.

Let me give you one vivid example. I once treated a gentleman who had been stabbed in the back a few days before during a knife fight. He returned to the emergency department

There is no one-size-fits-all approach to examining and treating people. Medicine and psychology, like spiritual care, are a combination of art and science.

because a large collection of fluid (a seroma) welled up under the sutures that had been placed in his back. It looked like he had a tennis ball under his skin.

I told him I'd need to drain the seroma. He had lain on his stomach when the doctor sewed him up a few days before. This time he was sitting up on the gurney while I got my instruments ready to treat him. When I began filling a syringe with Lidocaine, he became extremely agitated, jumped off the gurney screaming, and climbed up a cabinet toward the ceiling—just like Spiderman.

Imagine a fellow who got into knife fights being terrified of a one-inch needle the width of a human hair. However, scratch the psychic surface of someone like this, and you will invariably find that as a toddler they were held down and sewn up or had a similar traumatic episode during their impressionable youth.

There is value to exploring our past and the events that have led us to where we are today. Just like the man in the knife fight, we often are unaware of how past events continue to impact our mental well-being.

Again, humans are complicated, and there is no one-size-fits-all approach to examining and treating people. Medicine and psychology, like spiritual care, are a combination of art and science, and each case has to be taken on its own.

Below I've put together a brief overview of mental maladies that I hope will help you care for those in your life who may be struggling with depression and suicidal ideation. This overview isn't meant to be exhaustive, but I've found in my speaking to pastors that many are not trained to recognize basic mental disorders and are uncertain when to refer those in their care to mental health professionals for help.

The book that delineates the signs, symptoms, and diagnosis of mental disorders used by most US mental health practitioners is called *The Diagnostic and Statistical Manual of Mental Disorders*. It is now in its fifth edition (DSM-5). A hardbound copy is just shy of a thousand pages and a smidge over three pounds. Its production is overseen by the American

Psychiatric Association. The book was first published in 1952. Many complaints have been leveled at all the editions, but one only need look at the confusing Freudian-based psychiatric literature from the 1940s and 1950s to realize how useful it is for practitioners to agree on standards of nomenclature and diagnosis.

Many new diagnoses have been added to the DSM series over the years, and some have disappeared. When I was in grade school, we were taught that Pluto was the ninth planet in our solar system. In 2006, Pluto's status as a planet was revoked. Does that mean Pluto disappeared? No. Pluto is still in the Kuiper Belt out beyond the orbit of Neptune. Likewise, some of the conditions that were once listed in the DSM and have been removed are still out there and just as real as ever.

It's not necessary to carefully read every one of these descriptions, but I think it will be useful to at least skim these conditions. If one of them seems like it sheds light on a person you know and are trying to help, then, if desired, you can use the resources recommended in the appendixes to learn more.

A BRIEF OVERVIEW OF MENTAL MALADIES

Phobias

A phobia is an irrational fear that produces an avoidance response. (The gentleman I described earlier who had been in the knife fight had a phobia of needles.) Sometimes these responses can result in passing out or a panic attack. Phobias are one of the most common mental disorders in the population. A phobia may be of animals, bugs, thunderstorms, heights, or even death. Most do not require any treatment. When a phobia interferes with everyday life, however, it should be addressed.

Another type of phobia is the fear of a specific social setting. At the top of many people's list of things to avoid is speaking in public or meeting new people. It is sometimes difficult for those who have no mental illness to understand those who do. But many of us have a fear (if not a phobia) of heights or of speaking in public. If we can recall those feelings and multiply them times a hundred, we begin to get some insight and sympathy for those who have thoughts and feelings that they cannot control.

Anxiety Disorders

All of us have experienced anxiety. This happens when we meet a new challenge, like the first day of school or the first day on a new job. Imagine, however, if every day felt like the first day of school, and you will get an insight into anxiety disorders.

Two of the most common expressions of this category are panic disorder and agoraphobia. Both of these can occur after a traumatic event, such as a divorce. They manifest themselves as a feeling of foreboding or doom, accompanied by an increased pulse, sweating, or diarrhea. There are probably many who suffer from agoraphobia that we don't know about, simply because they don't go out much. Generalized anxiety disorders are experienced by twice as many women as men. Cognitive and behavioral therapies as well as medicines are used to help those with these disorders. Many anxiety disorders are successfully managed by primary care doctors. Several medical conditions can manifest with the symptoms of a generalized anxiety disorder, including caffeine intoxication, hyperthyroidism, and alcohol withdrawal.

Obsessive-Compulsive Disorders

Obsessive-compulsive disorders are very common. They affect men and women equally, and their rate of occurrence is fairly consistent across cultures. They are typified by an obsessive thought such as "Did I lock the door?" and the compulsion to check and recheck, even if it is for the fourth or fourteenth time. Interestingly, those who yield to the obsessive thoughts have a poorer prognosis than those who fight them. (Obsessive-compulsive disorder is different from an obsessive-compulsive personality, which we'll touch on later.) Obsessive-compulsive disorders can range from mild to debilitating. They may coexist with major depressive disorders.

Individuals may experience maladaptive reactions to acute stresses, such as witnessing or being involved in traumatic events. If the symptoms occur after an interval of time, it is called post-traumatic stress disorder (PTSD). The severity of the event is not as crucial as the individual's subjective response to the trauma. PTSD in combination with substance abuse or a major depression is a deadly combination. Perhaps one of the deadliest and most serious situations is one of individuals trying to cope with PTSD when the obsession is suicide.

Some 50 percent of those who commit suicide suffer from a mood disorder.

Major Thought Disorders

In many of the above disorders, an inciting trauma or incident can be identified. In the disorders we'll now discuss, the causative event seems to be more biological than experiential. These disorders are sometimes referred to as major thought disorders. Of these, schizophrenia is one of the most severe and seems to occur at the same rate across all cultures and periods of history. It has been estimated that as many as half of people who are chronically homeless have a diagnosis of schizophrenia. Schizophrenia is typified by incoherent and disorganized thinking, speech, and actions as well as the inability to distinguish reality from nonreality. The disease has several subtypes, such as paranoid, disorganized, and catatonic schizophrenia.

Suicide occurs in 10 percent of those suffering from schizophrenia. Some of the traits seen in schizophrenia manifest themselves in other mental disorders. If they are self-limited, they may be called a brief psychotic disorder (which often follows a severely stressful event). If the symptoms of schizophrenia are associated with a disturbance in mood, they may be termed a schizoaffective disorder, which involves a mixture of psychosis and a mood disorder.

Mood disorders are highly correlated to suicides. Some 50 percent of those who commit suicide suffer from a mood disorder.

The first variant of mood disorders we'll examine is called major depression, or major depressive disorder (MDD). It is twice as common in women as in men. It can occur after giving birth or may be seasonal, worsening in the fall and winter. Often no inciting incident can be identified.

A physician should screen a patient for medicines and other diseases that can mimic or cause depression. Anytime a patient starts a new medicine and depression develops subsequently, the medicine must be suspected of causing the depression. Everything from cancers to endocrine problems to infectious diseases can cause or mimic depression. Twice I recall patients presenting to the emergency department with a complaint of suicidal thoughts, and the cause turned out to be new antihypertensive medications. In another, it was undiagnosed sleep apnea; in another, hypothyroidism. This is why people should see their family doctor for the first episode of depression.

An excellent mnemonic for recognizing depression is SIG E CAPS. Each letter stands for a different facet of depression:

S = Sleep—either increased during the day or trouble sleeping at night

I = Interest—loss of interest in activities that used to give pleasure

G = Guilt—dwelling on regrets, or feelings of worthlessness

E = Energy—the lack thereof, or feelings of fatigue

C = Concentration—a decreased ability to think or concentrate

A = Appetite—usually reflected in weight loss or gain of over 5 percent

P = Psychomotor—increase in agitation or anxiety, slowing of thinking, and lethargy

S = Suicidal ideation—preoccupation with death and thoughts of suicide

We will explore this helpful tool more in chapter 8.

Not all depression presents in the same way. In some, mad equals sad. In other words, these patients do not show some of the typical depressive symptoms but will display difficulty getting along with others. In preteens and teens, the signs and symptoms may not be typical, or they may cycle rapidly between moods. In teens, look for a change from their norms. Be aware that most people who are depressed tend to isolate themselves. If someone elderly stops showing up, ask if they are feeling blue. The highest rate of suicide in our society is among widowed elderly males. But suicide can happen in any and all age groups. The city where I live had a ten-, eleven-, thirteen-, and fourteen-year-old commit suicide within the past year.

Research has shown that a combination of pharmacotherapy and psychotherapy together has been most effective in treating major depressive disorders. Treatments include selective serotonin reuptake inhibitors (SSRIs), tricyclic antidepressants (TCAs), monoamine oxidase inhibitors (MAOIs), and other atypical mood stabilizers, as well as electroconvulsive therapy (ECT). A psychiatrist may do genetic studies to determine a patient's propensity to metabolize neurotransmitters.

Bipolar Disorder
Another manifestation of mood disorders is bipolar disorder. The incidence of bipolar disorder (1 percent lifetime prevalence) is far less than that of unipolar, or major depressive, disorder. It is characterized by alternating mania and depression. Heredity seems to play a greater role in this variant of mood disturbance. In the manic stage, a patient can have racing, disorganized thoughts but may believe they are thinking better than ever. It is not uncommon for those in a manic state to spend excessively, use drugs (some 60 percent), stay up for days on end, or engage in risky behaviors, such as sex with strangers. Some may even experience hallucinations and other psychotic features.

Trying to stop a manic patient from doing what they want to can elicit a violent reaction. However, no matter how "out of it" someone may seem when they are manic, they should always be treated with dignity.

I once was called to see a patient in the ICU over a weeken. patient's nurse was quite helpful but acted a bit reticent around me. Whe I was through with the ICU patient, the nurse asked to speak with me. "Do you remember me?" she asked. I apologized that I didn't, making an excuse that I regularly worked in three hospitals in the area. She said that she'd had me for a doctor in the ER when she was in a manic episode. "You and the nurse on duty had to tackle me. But both of you were as kind as you could be. I appreciate it." The moral of the story is whether it is a friend, a relative, or a coworker, be respectful even when someone appears not to be able to think clearly. They are still humans. Most will get better. Someday they may be taking care of you. The first line of treatment for bipolar disorders is lithium, along with other mood stabilizers and electroconvulsive therapy (ECT).

Cognitive Disorders

These disorders represent difficulties with thinking, planning, and memory. They include delirium (short term), dementia (long term), and amnestic disorders. These maladies are typically worked up by family doctors and doctors in the emergency department. We'll not go into great detail here because they are less germane to our topic. However, keep in mind that some mental disorders can masquerade as dementia, most notably depression in the elderly, which presents as dementia or pseudo-dementia. It is a very satisfying thing to correctly diagnose a suspected dementia as a treatable and reversible depression.

Personality Disorders

Now let's look at the class of mental disorders known as personality disorders. These are disorders that may have a genetic component but also have a strong environmental element.

Personality disorders, unlike the thought disorders above, do not necessarily cause the person with them any distress. They are more likely to cause those around them distress. They are characterized by their

resistance to therapy and change. Inflexibility is the
comes to personality disorders. Confront someone
isorder for the hundredth time about some gap in their
ll often act as if it has never been mentioned.

nality disorders are associated with a higher suicide rate,
and _____ e of great interest to us. Although these disorders are known
to be notoriously difficult to treat or change, it has been my observation
that individuals who have them can be radically altered by faith and the
application of Christianity. For example, I know two people that meet the
classic criteria for narcissistic personality disorder. One is also an alcoholic
that has been sober for decades. Both are aware of their narcissism and have
consciously and conscientiously applied biblical principles to smooth over
the rough edges of their personality. Specifically, both spend vast amounts
of time and money helping others, with the understanding that this is the
path that God has made for them to become whole. By thinking less about
themselves and more about God's will for their lives, they grow healthy.
Indeed, whenever we humble ourselves before the Lord, all kinds of good
things can happen.

Personality disorders are generally divided into three broad groupings:
the odd or eccentric, the dramatic or emotional, and the anxious and fearful group. Much of what defines these various groupings are the defense
mechanisms used by those with the various disorders. I think this is why
Christianity is so effective with personality disorders. Christianity demands
that we put aside defense mechanisms such as splitting and denial.

Within a given group, it may be difficult to differentiate one personality disorder from another. This is why the disorders have traditionally
been left in groupings.

THE ODD/ECCENTRIC GROUP

The odd/eccentric group includes paranoid, schizoid, and schizotypal
personality disorders. Those with a paranoid personality disorder have a
pervasive distrust of others. They tend to be humorless and overconfident

and do not admit the need for others. They are litigious, appear and act angry, and are often suspicious.

Schizoid personalities appear aloof and indifferent to others. They seek solitary occupations, have little interest in emotional attachments, and do not seem to get much pleasure out of life. They are characterized by emotional coldness.

Schizotypal personality disorders resemble schizoid personalities, but they also have odd (i.e., magical) thoughts and sometimes paranoid ideation.

THE DRAMATIC/EMOTIONAL GROUP

The dramatic/emotional group includes borderline, histrionic, antisocial, and narcissistic personality disorders. Those with a borderline personality disorder are marked by unstable moods, relationships, and self-image. They may go from one sexual relationship or identity to another with little concern for others' feelings. They may shift rapidly from loving to hating someone. They are prone to use drugs, become depressed, and display self-destructive behaviors. They lie with remarkable ease and lack remorse when they are caught. At times they can be flirtatious and charming. Typically, they have had an explosive or abusive father. People with borderline personality disorder are at high risk for suicide, with some 10 percent dying in that manner. They frequently burn bridges behind themselves.

People with histrionic personality disorders are attention seekers, often being seductive. They are easily bored and fickle. They may focus on various illusive medical symptoms. Their expression of emotions is often dramatic and childish.

Those with an antisocial personality disorder have a basic disregard for the rights and feelings of others. They commonly come to the attention of the legal system. They frequently lie and have histories of cruelty to animals, truancy, and violence. They often abuse multiple drugs and are promiscuous.

Those with a narcissistic personality disorder have an exaggerated sense of self-worth and a diminished sense of others' worth. They believe they should be treated as special cases and that rules don't apply to them. They lack empathy and an understanding that others have feelings. They may react out of proportion if they believe someone hasn't respected them. They use denial and splitting. They are exploitive of others. They frequently lie and will refuse to own up when they are caught in a wrong. They often rewrite history to make themselves appear to be always right.

THE ANXIOUS/FEARFUL GROUP

The anxious/fearful group includes avoidant, dependent, obsessive-compulsive, and passive-aggressive personality disorders. As the name implies, those with avoidant personality disorders tend to avoid human contact. They are hypersensitive to rejection and have low self-esteem. They are pathologically shy and socially awkward.

People with a dependent personality disorder are more likely to be women. They avoid conflict and defer to others. Women may have a variant that is fused to a borderline personality. They have deep-seated feelings of inadequacy.

It has been estimated that 10 percent of those in the medical profession have obsessive-compulsive personality disorders. They tend toward perfectionism and are emotionally constricted, tidy, and notoriously stingy. They are often preoccupied with success at work to the detriment of human relationships. They have an intense dislike of losing control and are reluctant to share their feelings.

Passive-aggressive personality disorder is no longer listed in the DSM-5, but like Pluto, it is still out there. Our short list hasn't included many of the childhood disorders, or some of the more exotic conditions such as multiple personality disorders. But we have included many of the disorders that are associated with suicide.

IS THERE A CHRISTIAN WORLDVIEW OF MENTAL ILLNESS?

In the age before modern psychiatric terms, the concept of sin was inherent to understanding ourselves and others. In the world of the DSM-5, the concept of sin is nowhere to be found.

Previous to modern psychiatric diagnosis, many of the maladies above, particularly the personality disorders, were seen through the lens of vices and virtues. Traditionally, the seven deadly sins were balanced with the seven cardinal virtues that acted to combat them. Thus, lust was balanced by striving toward chastity, gluttony with temperance, greed with charity, sloth (or laziness) with diligence, wrath (or anger) with forgiveness, envy with kindness, and pride with humility.

As you review the diagnoses above, think about which ones are characterized by traits that would have been addressed in terms of sin in the past. Could a spiritual approach help? Are there virtues we can work toward to counteract some of our vices?

At the same time, consider how we started this chapter. People are complicated. The Christian worldview of mental illness needs to be equally nuanced. We must ask God for an extra measure of humility, self-examination, and grace as we interact with those suffering from any mental malady (including ourselves).

The physical, emotional, and spiritual are not separate entities. Christianity is the only faith in which our God took on a physical human form. Jesus suffered, wept, napped, feasted, celebrated, and was both tempted and betrayed. He knew how it felt to be a son and a brother, a friend and a leader, a teacher and a healer. As Christians, we should be sensitive to the interaction between the physical, emotional, and spiritual well-being of ourselves and within others. One rarely changes without impacting the other two.

PART 2

A Biblical Worldview of Suicide

The iron bolt which so mysteriously fastens
the door of hope and holds our spirits in gloomy prison,
needs a heavenly hand to push it back.

CHARLES SPURGEON

CHAPTER 5

Suicide and Satan

SATAN IS ALWAYS FOR DEATH

❋

A mighty fortress is our God, a bulwark never failing;
our helper he, amid the flood of mortal ills prevailing.
For still our ancient foe does seek to work us woe;
his craft and power are great, and armed with cruel hate,
on earth is not his equal.

MARTIN LUTHER

ONE MISERABLE, SLUSHY, GRAY WINTER DAY in the middle of a deep economic downturn, I walked out to my pickup truck. I was a carpenter back then, and there hadn't been much work in the trade, but I'd just gotten a job. As I slogged across the apartment parking lot to my truck, I got a nasty surprise. It wasn't there. The truck and all my tools were gone. Stolen. The wallet I'd left under the seat was gone. Everything I needed to make a living was gone. I was out of money. I had no family to ask for help.

Some days are like that. Some years are too. Life is full of disappointments. Sometimes just getting out of bed in the morning can leave you battered and bruised. Life isn't always fair. "The mass of men lead lives of quiet desperation," as Thoreau famously said. Many are closer to giving up than those around them realize. Unfortunately, we are not born with a road map to life in one hand and a compass in the other. We can spend decades climbing the ladder of success only to find that it is leaning against the wrong wall.

Similar to Dante's character in *The Divine Comedy*, many years later I too woke up in the middle of the journey of life only to find myself in the midst of a dark wood. I'd lost my way. The specifics are not important. What is important, and what is transferable, is the way out. I tried all the usual methods first: entertainment, accumulating things, and hiding from reality. Eventually, they stopped working—if they ever did.

I read the *Ramayana*, the *Bhagavad Gita*, and the Koran. Then I read the Bible. That's when I met Christ. I can't explain how sublime that first meeting was. "The Word became flesh" describes what happened when I realized that what I was reading in the pages of the Bible was *real*. But it is more than that. I realized that the main character in the two-thousand-year-old text I was reading was still alive. And *that*, my friends, is a truth stranger than fiction.

In our examination of the Bible and suicide, I'm not going to get into any of the fine points of theology that have divided Christians throughout the ages. Instead, I'll assume that those who claim the name of Christ (Christians) adhere to certain tenets of the faith that C. S. Lewis described as "mere Christianity." These are the beliefs that all Catholics, Eastern Orthodox, Coptic, and Protestant Christians hold in common. Fundamental to all is the belief that the Bible is the authoritative, sacred text of the faith. If we practice Christianity without holding the Bible as authoritative, we are really setting ourselves up as god. We are trying to ride piggyback on the legitimacy of Christianity, doing what we see fit, without the restraints imposed by the Bible. I mention this because we are entering the portion of this book where the Bible will clearly act as our ultimate guide.

The Bible isn't just about the folly of man and the love and sacrifice of Jesus. It also describes a malevolent force in the world. That force is still at work today. I saw the results of this wicked power in the emergency department. There is evil afoot in society, and it is real. It is the impetus behind every stolen truck, every murder, and every broken promise. Which brings us to the father of evil: Satan. If someone says they represent Christianity and does not acknowledge the reality and impact of Satan, they are fooling themselves and misleading others. Nothing in life makes sense without the Fall, and Satan is central to the Fall.

SATAN'S LIES TO ADAM AND EVE

With this in mind, let's open the Bible and see what it has to say about suicide. At the end of Creation, God was in heaven, man was in Paradise, and all was right with the universe. God gave Adam and Eve one rule: "Don't eat from the tree of the knowledge of good and evil, for in the day you eat of it, you will surely die."

"Got it! Check!" Adam and Eve chimed.

Then the Bible introduces a creature called the serpent. The serpent is described as being "more crafty" than any other creature (Genesis 3:1, ESV), subtle and underhanded unlike anything else on earth. Also known throughout the Bible as Satan, the devil, the beast, the adversary, and Beelzebub, the serpent is the enemy of God.

I once heard a comedian making fun of the story of the Fall. He laughed that the foe of mankind is described as a snake. I suspect he has never encountered a real one. The World Health Organization reports the grim results of the 5.4 million snakebites annually: 400,000 individuals are left with limbs amputated or disabled, and 100,000 die.

It's no surprise that the Bible would use this creature to typify our mortal foe. Snakes move rapidly and noiselessly. I recall several encounters with snakes in the grass beside various rivers. These aggressive, cold-blooded creatures come straight at you, fangs bared, determined to do harm. Wear boots, carry a stick, and walk a wide path around them—and Satan—is what the Bible is saying.

And so it was that long, long ago, Adam and Eve were tricked by a creature described as a serpent. The serpent promised that humans could be their own gods. They could be the measure of all things. They could determine right from wrong and good from evil. Something about that lie—and make no mistake, it was and is a lie—tempts us even to the present day.

Adam and Eve were told by God not to eat from one specific tree, but

Satan convinced them God was wrong. Satan called death "life," and evil "good." When Adam and Eve bought his lie, they pointed loaded revolvers to their temples.

They had been warned that the act would result in death, but they did it anyway. They swallowed all the tablets in the bottle; they held the razor blade to their wrist; they tied the last knot in the noose. They closed their eyes and stepped into an abyss. They committed suicide.

What we learn in the opening pages of the Bible is that God gives life and Satan takes it away. No other sacred text that I am aware of begins by telling humanity where the paradox that underlies the human condition comes from: that is, that we are attracted to the things that kill us. Unlike every other creature on earth, we are drawn toward things that we know will harm us.

I believe the Bible. It states that men and women are made in God's image. We are capable of making and guarding life. Yet we made a conscious decision to turn our backs on God and believe the serpent's lies. And so, history and our own experiences show that we are also capable of killing and destruction on a scale that can only be described as demonic. One of two forces can and will rule our lives. One creates life; the other destroys it. The question for you and me and for every human who has ever lived is this: Which side are you on? Remaining neutral isn't an option. If you decide to be a free agent, or don't choose a side, then by default, you have picked the side of Satan.[1]

God is light and truth. Satan represents death and lies. God calls us to the light. Satan calls us into shadows. Never is this brought more into focus than in the area of suicide. In which direction will we walk?

If only logic were at play, it would seem that we would always walk toward the light. But here is where the trickery begins. God calls light "light," and Satan calls darkness "light."[2]

The most consistent thing about Satan is that he does not tell the truth. Jesus calls Satan "the father of lies" (John 8:44). Satan is known for twisting the truth, obfuscating the truth, or insisting that a lie is the truth.

The opening of Genesis not only explains where suicide originated; it explains the loneliness that every one of us feels.

Through deception, deceit, and falsehood, Satan gains a foothold in our lives, our brains, and our thoughts. Without some sort of compass pointing toward truth, it is hard for us to tell the difference between truth and lies. This battle between truth and lies, life and death, light and darkness is as old as humanity.

First impressions are important. In the opening chapters of Genesis, Satan convinces humanity to trade Paradise for thorns and thistles, immortality for three score and ten, and life for death. In short, Satan was on the scene of the first suicide, telling us to swallow the poison.

God made a compromise and a concession with Adam and Eve. They did not die the day they ate from the tree of the knowledge of good and evil. Instead, he made them mortal beings. He evicted them from the Garden of Eden. Adam and Eve may have dodged the immediate bullet, but all who have come after them are still paying the price for their folly. Oh, to be able to walk naked and unashamed with our Father and Creator in the cool of the day again!

We humans were designed and built to run on a relationship with our Maker. Before the Fall, the relationship between God and us was probably similar to that of a loving parent and child, only a thousand times better. After the Fall, we were separated from God. Thus, the opening of Genesis not only explains where suicide originated; it explains the loneliness that every one of us feels.

Each of us must decide how we will deal with this loneliness. Will we seek to reestablish our relationship with God? Will we make *ourselves* god? Will we place another person on that throne? Or will we live our lives in pursuit of power, pleasure, or possessions? We looked at some of these roads to meaning in chapter 1, and the Bible shows us what happens when any of these options are chosen, so we don't have to ruin our lives by actually going down the various paths ourselves.

God has a deep love for us. He sent his only Son to rescue us. We cannot love God and fail to love what he loves. Inherent in loving God is a concern for other people, our neighbors.

When Satan first showed up in the Bible, he convinced Adam and Eve to kill themselves. He convinced humanity to give up Paradise and sever our relationship with God. If anyone hears a voice telling them to commit suicide, it is important to know that that voice never comes from God. It has been Satan's calling card since day one.

SATAN AND JOB

What does Satan do when he shows up again in the Bible? Let's turn to the book of Job to find out. Job is either the oldest or the second oldest book in the Bible. Literary scholars love this book. It is a gem. Biblical scholars call it a book about theodicy, which means it's a book about how and why a good God allows evil to exist.

To be honest, why God allows evil to exist is not a subject I've wrestled with much. It has been clear to me since I first believed that if God were to subtract all evil from the world, I'd be high on the list to go. Only a fool or a narcissist would think that a perfectly just God would make a special exception just for them.

Instead of looking at Job to answer why bad things happen to good people, let's read it from a different angle that suits our discussion of suicide. Because at its heart, Job is the story of Satan trying to convince the best of humanity to turn his back on the source of life: God. Or, as Job's wife (who acts as the "Greek chorus" in the book) puts it, to "curse God and die." If we read it that way, we can discern the qualities that help fend off Satan and prevent suicide.

The book opens by telling us how fortunate Job is. He has great standing in the community and lives in what was probably the best neighborhood on the planet. He and his wife have raised successful adult children who all get along. He has his health. He has enormous wealth. He has friends. He fears God. He is honest. He avoids evil. He helps the poor.

Lastly, he believes in the fundamental goodness of God. He lives in the faith that he will someday—even after he is long dead—see God in the flesh.

What can we learn from this list of what Job has and believes? If the book of Job shows us how to successfully stand against Satan's lies, then we should pay close attention to the qualities that give Job strength, even when Satan throws his worst against him.

Essentials versus Nonessentials for Resiliency

First, the nonessentials. Satan believed that Job's high regard for God was solely the result of the nonessentials—his health, wealth, and standing in the community. God allowed Satan to test this hypothesis. One by one, Satan takes the nonessentials from Job. Satan's goal is to get Job to curse God (the opposite of fearing God). This is his goal for all of us. He's also perfectly happy to have us eat the poisoned fruit, or swallow the sleeping pills, or pull the trigger that leads to our death.

One after another, horrible things happen to Job. He loses his wealth and his health. He loses the love and support of his wife and his friends. He loses his reputation. He even loses his beloved children—perhaps the hardest test of all. But with all these misfortunes, Job does not, as the Bible poetically describes suicide, "curse God and die."

Why didn't Job just give up? Because he had qualities that no one can take away, not even Satan himself. These essentials include honesty, hope, and faith. Job was honest with himself, others, and God. Some translations say he was "blameless and upright" (Job 1:1, ESV). He feared the Lord and shunned evil.

For most of us, if we're honest, health, wealth, standing, and family are placed (and pursued) above honesty, fear of the Lord, and avoidance of sin. This is perhaps why despair and suicide attempts often come in the wake of losing something. Perhaps a medical test comes back bearing bad news. Or we are fired from our job. Or we are caught cheating on our taxes or on our spouse and lose our reputation in the community. Or a child dies, or a son or daughter refuses to speak with us ever again.

Job experiences many of these same losses (and others not on this list), yet he does not succumb to Satan's temptation. He doesn't lose faith in God. And while he seems on the brink of despair, he does not commit suicide. Why? Because Job knows the difference between essentials and nonessentials. He understands the difference between what can be taken away and what is eternal. And he discerns the difference between God's truth and Satan's lies.

Discerning Truth from Lies

At some points, the book of Job is tedious. Job's "friends" spend chapter after chapter accusing Job of sins that he has not committed. It's interesting to note that the word *Satan* means "accuser." For most of the book, Job's friends act on the devil's behalf—they play the role of devil's advocate.

Three of Job's friends flat out have bad theology. Eliphaz believes in his "prosperity gospel," that God rewards good behavior with material comforts; Bildad believes that everything bad that befalls us is the result of unconfessed sin, so Job's current troubles are the result of past sins; and Zophar leans too far in the direction known today as hyperreformism— we are God's puppets, so any actions we take are ultimately meaningless. Lastly, Job's young friend Elihu seems to have his theology right, but he has forgotten that without love, perfect theology doesn't reflect who God is.

The key to decoding what are lies and what is true in the book of Job is God's response to Job. God doesn't comment on young Elihu, but he does say that what Job's three other friends have said is dead wrong.[3]

In the end, Job's fame, fortune, family, and reputation are restored to him. But what is it that kept Job from committing suicide when he had lost everything and was covered with pus-oozing sores from head to toe? How is it that when Job's own wife tells him to curse God and commit suicide that Job can say, "The LORD gave, and the LORD has taken away; blessed be the name of the LORD" (Job 1:21, ESV)?

Job's resiliency is grounded in something we don't speak about much these days: fear of the Lord. The Bible says that "fear of the LORD is the foundation of wisdom. Knowledge of the Holy One results in good judgment" (Proverbs 9:10). Job has both respect and fear for someone who can speak a universe into being. Job believes that God made him and that all life is a gift from the Lord.

Over the last century, some have portrayed God as a domesticated, doddering buddy who just wants to take us out for ice cream. While God always wants what is best for us, he is so much more than our buddy. He is the all-powerful, all-knowing Lord, ever constant, infinitely just, and holy. The Bible tells us that God is slow to anger and quick to forgive—neither capricious nor arbitrary—always trying to grow us in his ways.

More to the point, God is our Father in heaven—and on earth. In fact, God in his role as Father does one thing for his children that is not spoken of in society much today, even in church: God punishes his children. Why? Because he loves us.

Our society has trouble with the concept of parents punishing their children. I recall the first time I heard someone put a name to what parenting without punishment is. Our team was on pediatric rounds one morning with the most brilliant doctor I've ever worked with. He was a pediatrician. We had just examined a three-year-old child with second- and third-degree burns. The child had sustained her injuries when her mother was present in the room cooking. The child wanted to be up on the counter, "helping." Initially, Mom said no. Then the child started to cry, so Mom acquiesced and lifted the child up to the cooking area of the counter. The child knocked over a boiling pot, scalding herself.

As the mother expressed regret, one of the residents was quick to assuage her guilt. As soon as our team was back out in the hallway, the attending physician came down hard on the resident. "Your generation will have to deal with two types of child abuse. The first kind is straightforward. Those are the children whose parents are harsh and capricious. The second kind is the permissive parent who never punishes their children." He pointed back to the patient exam room. "That child's parents are guilty of child abuse."

Hebrews 12 expands on the subject of God punishing us when we need it. The author asks, "Who ever heard of a child who is never disciplined by its father?" (Hebrews 12:7). Fast-forward to our generation, and these parents are quite prevalent. As a result, many today suffer because they didn't learn critical lessons when the cost was relatively inexpensive. Moreover, they have a corrupted view of what discipline really is: the hard work of parenting.

The implication of this permissiveness is that we no longer consider God—or even ourselves—as the cause behind some of the hard times we are going through. Did I lose my job because God called me into another less lucrative or glamorous occupation and I didn't obey? (Consider the story of Jonah.) Is my heart broken because my significant other dumped me, or because I didn't listen to God and steer clear of that person in the first place? (Consider the stories of David and Bathsheba or Samson and Delilah.)

According to the wisdom in Hebrews, if we can't point to hard times that we have experienced because God sent them to punish us, then we can't claim to be children of God. "For the LORD disciplines those he loves, and he punishes each one he accepts as his child" (Hebrews 12:6).

In the case of Job, Job is not being punished for wrongs done. But Job is an exception. Most of us should ask if a trial we are going through is God punishing us because he loves us and wants to keep us from an even greater consequence: "Is God giving me a swat on the backside because he loves me and doesn't want me to get run over in the road by sin?" If that is the case, hard times and suffering take on a new and divine meaning and are not just something to be avoided. "God's discipline is always good for us, so that we may share in his holiness. No discipline is enjoyable while it is happening—it's painful! But afterward there will be a peaceful harvest of right living for those who are trained in this way" (Hebrews 12:10-11).

In addition to resiliency based on fear of the Lord, Job possesses another virtue that is in short supply today—a quality I wish I had more of. When someone is being tested to the limits but remains calm, we say they have "the patience of Job."[4] Job had patience in spades. Remember our discussion earlier about the importance of language and the relationship between the noun and the adjective "patient"? A good patient trusts. Because a physician sees thousands of patients, he or she has a much larger pool of experience when it comes to treating diseases. Instead of experiencing one cancer, the oncologist has the perspective of thousands. No matter what misfortunes Satan throws at Job, he never loses his patient trust in God and the humility to believe that God is bigger, wiser, and more powerful than he will ever understand.

The Bible tells us that God can raise us from the dead. Job lives in this hope and clings to it like a man in a nighttime storm clings to a life raft. Sometimes all we have left is hope, but this is enough, because this kind of hope always wins.

It is not a hope based on *our* strengths and weaknesses. It is a hope based on God. As Job puts it, "But as for me, I know that my Redeemer lives, and he will stand upon the earth at last. And after my body has decayed, yet in my body I will see God! I will see him for myself. Yes, I will see him with my own eyes. I am overwhelmed at the thought!" (Job 19:25-27).

SATAN AND THE TEMPTATION OF CHRIST

Both in Genesis and Job, Satan tries to get people to sever their relationships with God and kill themselves in the process. In the New Testament, Satan goes toe to toe with Jesus. This is the episode known as the temptation of Christ.

When Satan tempted Adam and Eve, he did so in the setting of Paradise, where they were surrounded by food. When Satan tempts Jesus, it is in the opposite setting: the wilderness. This is not an accident. Jesus faces the same foe, but in much more trying circumstances. And yet Jesus succeeds where Adam and Eve failed. Why? Because Jesus is the new Adam, who came to fix what Adam messed up. The author of life faces the author of death and wins.

Having fasted for forty days, Jesus is hungry. So Satan tempts Jesus with food. Jesus responds by quoting Scripture: "It is written, 'Man shall not live by bread alone'" (Luke 4:4, ESV).

Next, Satan tempts Jesus by offering him all the kingdoms of the world. "It's all yours for the asking," Satan says, "if you will only worship me." Jesus counters, "It is written, 'You shall worship the Lord your God, and him only shall you serve'" (Luke 4:8, ESV).

Lastly, Satan puts Jesus on a high tower and says, "Jump! Angels will catch you!" To this, Jesus responds, "It is said, 'You shall not put the Lord your God to the test'" (Luke 4:12, ESV).

Jesus responds to Satan's temptations with three counterattacks. First, that God is the sole source of spiritual nourishment. Second, that God alone is worthy of worship. And third, that God alone decides when he will bend the laws of his universe to rescue us with a miracle. It is important for us to notice that Adam listened to Satan's lies while Jesus listened to God's truth. Jesus relied on God and God alone (demonstrated by his understanding and applying Scripture) to successfully resist Satan's lies.

> *Adam listened to Satan's lies while Jesus listened to God's truth.*

In short, we should live by faith. We should never give up our hope in the Lord. But we must not demand or expect that God do our bidding.

It is a curious thing that even though Satan makes so few personal appearances in Scripture, each time he does, he is trying to get someone to kill themselves or someone else. As we see throughout the Bible, Satan is always for death.[5] We will see this pattern continue in our last example: Judas Iscariot.

SATAN AND JUDAS

Satan interacts with one more major character in Scripture, Judas Iscariot. Judas was picked by Jesus to be one of his twelve disciples. For three years Judas followed Jesus of Nazareth on his mission. He witnessed Jesus walk on water, feed five thousand, heal the sick, raise the dead, and preach the gospel.

Yet something was wrong with Judas. His eye couldn't see well even when he was staring right at Goodness itself. What was wrong with Judas? I'm going to make a guess, but first follow me as I head down a rabbit trail once again. Be patient: I promise that this trail is germane to our understanding of Satan and suicide.

If you ask the average Christian what happened to Paul on the road to Damascus, they will tell you that Paul fell off his horse. But just like the apple that Eve ate, Paul's horse is not in the Bible. Why do people believe that Paul fell off his horse? Because one of the greatest religious painters of all time depicted the scene that way. Four hundred years ago Caravaggio painted *Conversion on the Way to Damascus*, and he shows Paul thrown to the ground with his horse above him. It is a masterpiece. Part of Caravaggio's genius was to see a truth in the Bible that wasn't necessarily noted in the text.

Likewise, Caravaggio painted *The Taking of Christ*, which depicts the scene of Judas betraying Jesus in the garden of Gethsemane. Here we see Judas reaching out to plant a kiss on Jesus' cheek and Jesus recoiling, as if in disgust. Judas has coarse features. His eyes are bloodshot. Jesus draws away as one draws away from the breath of a drunk. Like Rembrandt, Caravaggio paints his own weaknesses on the characters in his religious paintings. Caravaggio struggled with his temper and alcohol, and so he painted Judas as a drunk.

Now, while Judas's drinking is conjecture, we know for certain from the Bible that Judas was a liar, a traitor, and a thief. He stole from money donated to help Jesus in his ministry.[6] What did he spend the money on? Caravaggio gives us one possible answer: alcohol.

In Scripture, we find that "Satan entered into Judas" (Luke 22:3), and the result is that Judas betrays his friends and the Lord. He sells out Jesus for thirty pieces of silver—the price of a slave. Before Jesus is put to death, Judas recants and attempts to return the money he was given for betraying Jesus. But there is no stopping the train of events that Judas set in motion. Distraught, Judas hangs himself. Apparently, his body stayed where it was, because no one took it down until it had decomposed enough to fall on the ground and burst open.[7]

What was wrong with Judas? He had the privilege of living next to the Son of God, witnessing miracles that few in the history of humanity ever have the honor to see, and nonetheless he took his own life. Why? In short, he listened to Satan's lies rather than God's truth.

Unlike Job, Judas did not discern between the essentials and the non-essentials. He did not cultivate the qualities that no one can take away—virtues such as honesty, patience, hope, and faith. Unlike Jesus, he did not arm himself with biblical truth so he would remain strong despite trying circumstances. Weakened by greed and pride, Judas—like Adam and Eve—succumbed to Satan's temptations and committed one of the most famous suicides in history.

WHAT SATAN TEACHES US ABOUT SUICIDE

I've not given an exhaustive biblical survey of Satan. Suffice it to say that every time Satan turns up, death isn't far behind. For example, when Satan shows up next in the Bible, he causes a husband and wife to commit perjury with mortal consequences.[8] The pattern is clear and consistent throughout Scripture: Satan is full of lies. When we believe his lies, death ensues.

Life is hard. Sometimes we lead lives of quiet desperation. But no matter what calamitous circumstances are facing us, we can hold firmly to this truth: Jesus is for life. Satan is always on the side of death—either directly or through the hopelessness, desperation, and choices he encourages that lead to death.

Knowing the difference between Satan's lies and God's truth is the definition of wisdom.

When you or your loved one is in a season of great suffering, when your truck and tools and wallet all go missing and you wonder how you can possibly pay the rent or scrounge up the next meal, remember Thoreau's less famous line: "The mass of men lead lives of quiet desperation. . . . But it is a characteristic of wisdom not to do desperate things."

CHAPTER 6

God and Suicide

JESUS IS ALWAYS FOR LIFE

❊

Amazing Grace, how sweet the sound
That saved a wretch like me
I once was lost but now am found
Was blind, but now, I see.

JOHN NEWTON

NOT LONG AGO, I was speaking on the subject of suicide in front of a group of about 150 men. During my talk, I read aloud from the adventures of the apostle Paul as recorded in the sixteenth chapter of the book of Acts. Paul and his wingman, Silas, had just finished a tough day in the city of Philippi. They'd been beaten and thrown in jail, and not just in the general holding cell. They had been put in stocks and locked inside an inner, super-secure cell.

However, this didn't slow down Paul and Silas. Around midnight, after singing some songs, Paul began preaching and praying up a storm. Well, technically, what Paul preached up was not a storm, but a seismic event. The ground literally began to shake. (Earthquakes were common to the area; Philippi was eventually destroyed by an earthquake in AD 619.) The cell walls cracked, the stocks broke apart, and the lanterns were extinguished.

The warden, arriving in darkness and confusion, saw the prison doors hanging off their hinges. As the dust settled, he surmised that the earth-quake had allowed all the prisoners to escape. He was doomed. The city council would be furious. He drew his sword and was ready to fall on it rather than face the consequences of the jailbreak.

Paul and Silas knew that if the inmates stayed quiet a minute longer, their jailer would commit suicide. Then the prisoners could really escape!

Pausing for effect, I leaned forward on the podium and asked my audience, "What would you do if you were Paul?"

Silence.

I looked several men sitting in the front row right in the eye and then confessed, "I don't know about you, but I'd be tempted to keep my mouth shut."

Unlike some audiences, this group seemed to have no problem turning back the clock two thousand years and imagining themselves in Paul's shoes. Perhaps that's because all of us were behind high walls, razor wire, and multiple guard stations. I was speaking to these men in a maximum-security prison. It took me two hours to drive there. The prison is in the middle of nowhere, and guests are few and far between. In fact, on my second visit, just by walking up to the podium, I received a standing ovation.

I'd come to talk with these men about God and suicide, and to listen to them. The suicide rate among incarcerated men and women is higher even than in the general population. Every prison, like every church, includes people who have much to be ashamed of, much to regret, and many chances to despair. The wise ones seek forgiveness. They know that the only way to receive absolute forgiveness is to throw their lot in with Christ.

It is not uncommon to come across inmates in their fifties or sixties serving life sentences who first met the Lord in prison in their twenties. Like cloistered monks, they have spent decade after decade studying the Bible in cells. When you've learned how to cope with depression, conquer despair, and wake up every day looking for what the Lord would have you do, *while* doing a life sentence, you've got hold of one thing folks on the outside can never buy.

Still, no one spoke up. "Think about it," I prompted. "All you have to do is keep quiet, and you're out the door." The men glanced at each other and then over to my friend, the prison chaplain.

"Well, I might have been tempted to keep quiet," I continued, "but when Jesus is in the house, people don't kill themselves. They live."

Just then a guard came into the room and whispered in the chaplain's ear. The chaplain stood up. "Okay, everybody, we're on lockdown," he said. The men waited in line to shake my hand, thanked me, and then quietly returned to their cells.

For the next two hours, I was locked in prison too. I called my wife to let her know I'd been delayed, then pondered the irony of my situation. It wasn't clear to me if God had just given me a wink, a dummy slap, or an amen, yet I *knew* with certainty that the Lord had been in that room, *with* us.

Two thousand years ago, God certainly was there in the Philippian jail. When Paul realized that their captor was going to kill himself, he called out in a loud voice, "Stop! Don't kill yourself! We are all here!" (Acts 16:28). Startled by Paul's words, the jailer called for a lantern, rushed into the inner cell, and fell trembling before Paul and Silas. Then the warden asked the key question, the question everyone should ask—especially anyone who has been in despair and come so close to killing themselves: "Sirs, what must I do to be saved?" (Acts 16:30).

Paul and Silas answered, "Believe in the Lord Jesus and you will be saved, along with everyone in your household!" (Acts 16:31). What a perfect answer, and what a beautiful answer it is today: "Believe in the Lord Jesus!"

This brings us to the question of this chapter: What does God think of suicide?

Was Paul, God's man on the scene in the jail at Philippi, acting in accord with the Lord's wishes when he stopped the jailer from killing himself? The short and the long answer is yes! In preventing a suicide, Paul was both acting fully in accordance with God's will and witnessing for Jesus.

More than one character in the Bible has voiced a desire to end it all. We can learn what God thinks about suicide by examining what happened when these people made their intentions known to the Lord. A clear pattern emerges, which reinforces the message of Paul to the Philippian jailer.

MOSES THROWING IN THE TOWEL

The first case we'll consider is Moses. Of all the people in the Bible, Moses was given one of the toughest jobs. Tasked with defying the leader of the longest-running civilization on earth and leading a group of people who had been enslaved for centuries, Moses is given an almost impossible assignment: teach the newly freed slaves to live like God's people. If Moses turns his back for a moment, however, his charges start partying like students on spring break. They constantly complain about the difficulty of wilderness living. And Moses can't even rely on his brother and sister to stand firm in their support. To make matters worse, the Hebrew people don't care for his wife, who is an outsider.

Facing tremendous pressure and at the end of his wits, Moses cries out to God, "Why don't you just kill me if you're going to treat me like this?"[1] God hears Moses' cry and springs into action. To ease the burden, God sends seventy elders to take on some of Moses' responsibilities. He corrals and punishes Moses' brother and sister. He answers the people's demand for meat and feeds them quail. In short, once Moses tells God that he doesn't want to live, God sets things in motion to rescue him. This is a pattern that is repeated throughout the Bible.

ELIJAH CALLING IT QUITS

Elijah is another of the Lord's servants who cries out that he's at the end of his rope. No prophet in Israel was more impressive than Elijah. In partnership with God, Elijah stopped the rains from falling for three and a half years, was fed by ravens, and helped feed a widow and her son during a prolonged drought. He raised a boy from the dead. He took on and defeated hundreds of the prophets of the infant-sacrificing god Baal. And what a show it was! During his ministry, he called down fire from the Lord—not once, not twice, but thrice. Elijah accomplished these things during the reign of one of his country's worst kings, Ahab, *and* the wicked queen Jezebel.

One day, after Jezebel threatens Elijah's life, the exhausted prophet flees into the wilderness and collapses in the shade of a juniper tree. Hungry, alone, and discouraged, Elijah tells God that he wants to die. Everything appears dark and foreboding. It is not that the prophet hasn't done and seen great things. It is not that he has been let down by the Lord. Elijah simply seems to have worn himself out.

In the shade of the tree, Elijah falls asleep. The Lord sends an angel, who tenderly touches the prophet. "Arise and eat," the angel says (1 Kings 19:5, ESV), and in front of Elijah is warm bread and sweet water. Elijah eats and drinks and then falls back to sleep. Again, the angel of the Lord touches the prophet and provides a meal. Again, Elijah eats fresh bread and drinks.

Feeling somewhat refreshed, Elijah heads to a cave.

"Go out and stand before me on the mountain," the LORD told him. And as Elijah stood there, the LORD passed by, and a mighty windstorm hit the mountain. It was such a terrible blast that the rocks were torn loose, but the Lord was not in the wind. After the wind there was an earthquake, but the Lord was not in the earthquake. And after the earthquake there was a fire, but the Lord was not in the fire. And after the fire there was the sound of a gentle whisper. When Elijah heard it, he wrapped his face in his cloak and went out and stood at the entrance of the cave.

1 KINGS 19:11-13

I'd like to use the story of Elijah to highlight four biblical lessons that will help us in our discussion of suicide.

Lesson #1: Even God's Best Can Despair

The first lesson is that even God's best can grow despondent. Elijah is a super prophet. No one can compete with Elijah when it comes to propheting. He's the original fire-and-brimstone preacher. But he's also human. Believing he is the only faithful servant of the Lord left in Israel—even though there are seven thousand others he's unaware of—he feels abandoned. He's hungry. He's angry. He's lonely. He's worn down.

When our children were young and getting bent out of shape, my wife, Nancy, and I trained them to stop and do a systems check. To help them remember, we taught them the acronym HALT. Were they frustrated, sad, or not getting along because they were hungry, angry, lonely, or tired—i.e., HALT? Learning to pause and identify the underlying root of the problem helped our children take a deep breath and identify solutions.

For years, I worked twenty-four-hour shifts. At the end of a shift, I could still take care of sick patients, but that was all. If people pressed me for an answer on anything other than patient care, I learned to say, "That will have to wait until after I've slept, showered, shaved, and eaten."

We all can fall into despair, but sometimes the solution is as simple as meeting our basic needs. So let me pause here and offer some practical advice: no matter what age you are, if you haven't learned to do a HALT systems check, start now. Likewise, if you are a parent, teacher, church leader, or friend, teaching others to HALT, especially before making any consequential decision, can be a great gift. So many of our regrettable actions (including suicide) take place when we are under one or more of these four attacks.

Elijah was distraught because he felt all four deficits at once: hunger, anger, loneliness, and exhaustion. God recognized the causes of his hopelessness and ministered accordingly.

Lesson #2: Being Hungry, Angry, Lonely, and Tired Can Kill You

The second lesson of Elijah is that being chronically hungry, angry, lonely, or tired can kill you. It can lead to depression and suicidal thinking. For example, one of the many factors contributing to our current teen suicide crisis, I believe, is their erratic sleep schedule. Because of social media, constant communication, and the fear of missing out, many teens never get more than a few hours of uninterrupted sleep. Deep Rapid Eye Movement sleep (REM) is necessary for maintaining positive mental health. Learning to stop and take a HALT assessment (and do remediation, like turning off our electronic devices or placing them in another room) is a skill that should be cultivated from an early age. (We'll look at how to improve sleep hygiene more in chapter 8.)

Lesson #3: God Speaks to Us in the Quiet

The third lesson found in the story of Elijah is that often God speaks to us when we are at rest. We rarely hear the voice of the Lord in our busyness. More often, his soft voice comes out of the stillness. "Be still, and know that I am God!" the Lord says (Psalm 46:10). A life without regular quiet interludes is too noisy to hear the voice of the Lord. Over the past two thousand years, Western civilization has lived with a pattern of resting one day out of every seven. Ours is the first generation to go without this life-giving pattern of rest and work, and it is not going well. (We'll discuss this further when we get to part 3.)

Lesson #4: You Don't Have to Do It Alone

Our fourth lesson comes after the episode where Elijah wanted to die. Elijah can no longer shoulder the burden alone, so he calls out to God. To lessen the load, God assigns Elijah three less difficult tasks: he is to anoint two new kings and to choose his successor.[2] Here we see a similarity between how God helped Elijah and how God helped Moses. Sometimes we are trying to do too much by ourselves. It is a sign of wisdom and strength,

It is a sign of wisdom and strength, not weakness, to ask the Lord for guidance.

not weakness, to ask the Lord for guidance. Help in the form of turning things over to others, delegating, or reassignment might be in order to pull us back from the brink of despair.

JONAH'S DEATH WISH

Another prophet who wanted to end his life was Jonah. Jonah was instructed by the Lord to travel to Nineveh, the capital city of Israel's great enemy Assyria. He was to tell those in the city to repent of their evil ways; otherwise, in forty days God would destroy their city.

Destroying the city of Nineveh is exactly what Jonah wanted God to do. So Jonah gets on a boat and heads in the opposite direction. You probably know the story. The boat carrying Jonah in the wrong direction hits foul weather. The crew senses that this is the doing of a deity. Jonah confesses that he has rebelled against the Lord and that his disobedience is the cause of the storm. The crew of the foundering boat throw Jonah overboard, and the seas grow calm. Jonah is swallowed by a whale. I believe that when he was swallowed, he died. As his soul is "fainting away" (Jonah 2:7, ESV), Jonah calls out to the Lord. The Lord rescues and resurrects Jonah, and the whale spits out his body.[3]

It's pretty hard to ignore being thrown into a raging sea, swallowed by a whale, dying, being brought back to life, and then spat out on a sunny, Mediterranean beach. So when God again commands Jonah to preach repentance to the capital city of the Assyrians, Jonah gets his bearings straight and goes. Jonah enters the massive walled city and begins to cry out, "Repent, or in forty days the Lord is going to turn this place into a parking lot!" And repent they do. The king gets off his jewel-encrusted throne, takes off his dazzling silk robes, and puts on rags. He sits on the ground in an ash heap and asks the Lord to spare them. Everyone follows suit. They fast. They close their payday loan shops, bars, casinos, and fight clubs, and they cry aloud to the Lord.

What does the Lord do? The Lord spares Nineveh. How does Jonah react? He gets mad. He pitches a hissy fit. "I knew you were slow to anger and quick to forgive. I knew you were merciful and kind," Jonah whines. "I should have just stayed home. I don't want to live anymore." Jonah goes out of the city, sits down, and pouts.

Why is Jonah so bent out of shape? The gap between his expectations (that God would destroy Nineveh) and reality (God spared Nineveh) is too great for him to bear. I think that 90 percent of all human frustration is a result of the gap between our expectations and reality.

So the Lord decides to teach Jonah a lesson. He makes a plant to grow rapidly over Jonah to shade him from the hot sun. Jonah is pleased with the plant and the shade it provides. But the next day, as the sun rises, the Lord causes the plant to die. The unrelenting heat and sun beat down on Jonah. Again, Jonah is angry. He is hot, and he has lost his shade. He tells God he doesn't want to live. "Really?" God says. "You're so upset about a plant that you want to die, and you weren't even worried about a city with 120,000 little children who can't tell their left hand from their right? And what about all the innocent animals in the city?"

Like Jonah, I find it hard to pray for my enemies; I'd rather the Lord smite them. Too often, we who believe in the Lord want to act as the world's prosecutor, judge, and jury. In Jonah's case, it led him to a suicidal state of mind. God, however, doesn't want us to commit suicide. Nor does he want us to be the prosecutor, judge, or jury of others. In other words, God doesn't want us to take his job. He wants us to be witnesses of who he is and what he has done for us. When Jonah wanted to die, God used creation to teach him a lesson that shifted his perspective.

JESUS AND SUICIDE

So far as I am aware, there is no instance in the Bible where someone is recorded as saying to the Lord, "I no longer want to live" and the Lord does not stop them. God may take away some of their work, give them helpers, reassign them, or even point out how foolish they are being. Regardless of whether they are Moses, David, Job, or Jonah, God wants them to live.

What about when the Lord's Son walked the face of the planet? In

John's Gospel, Jesus said that if you had seen him, you have seen his Father. If you've heard him, you've heard his Father.

From the very outset of this book, we have established that suicide is a phenomenon that separates us from all other creatures on this planet. Suicide makes no sense. Yet humans aren't just suicidal as individuals; we are suicidal on a far greater scale. As we established earlier, the human race began by ignoring a warning and knowingly doing something that led to physical and spiritual death. Suicide doesn't just separate us from creation. It, like all sin, separates us from our Creator. God can forgive any sin and bring us into his presence for eternity. But sin is like fire; it is best to avoid touching it in the first place.

Indeed, Christ came to *save* humanity from itself. Jesus put it succinctly in Luke 19:10: "The Son of Man came to seek and to save the lost" (ESV). In fact, Jesus illustrates what our reaction to mental illness and even death should be. Allow me to detour for a moment and illustrate how I've seen God work today in this area.

Jesus Is Still Healing the Hopeless

One of the first churches our family was involved with supported permanent missionaries in Honduras. Medical teams from our church would go several times a year and spend two weeks holding clinics hosted by the permanent missionaries. My friend John, a superb family doctor, frequently led those trips.

Doctors' offices from around the state donated supplies to the effort. Boxes of antibiotics, inhalers, vitamins, and bandages arrived. To transport all the supplies, each person going on the mission brought one suitcase of their own personal belongings and one suitcase filled with medicines.

In addition to the antibiotics and other commonly used drugs, for one particular trip John was given a very large supply of an expensive, atypical antipsychotic drug. It was not the kind of drug that would characteristically be distributed from an open-air clinic held in the mountains on the border of Honduras and Nicaragua. At first the antipsychotics were packed, and then taken out. Then another person signed on for the trip, and the drug was repacked, only to be removed again when John received a donation of more useful drugs. And so it went, until the medicines had been packed and unpacked three times.

John then had the distinct impression that, practical or not, God wanted the antipsychotics to go with the team. The drugs were repacked for the fourth time and the team left. For a week, while holding clinics, John wondered at the wisdom of bringing the antipsychotic drugs. Then a family came and asked if the team might send someone to look at a woman in her twenties who was dying.

The woman, Araceli, lived in a mud and thatch hut. Although in her early twenties, she weighed about sixty pounds. She lay in a contracted fetal position. She was nonverbal. Her only activity was to bang her head against the wall, which she'd worn a hole through. She was covered in filth and refused to wear clothes or eat food. Her distressed parents were resigned to her imminent death. They had lost two other children around the same age from the same mysterious malady.

Was it cancer? A degenerative neurologic disease? Chronic heavy metal toxicity? Batten disease? Huntington's?

"If ever there was a woman possessed by seven demons, I was looking at her," John said. Perhaps this was schizophrenia. The diagnosis, much less treatment with the drug, was uncertain. However, she was going to die within days if left untreated, and Providence had seen to it that the team had antipsychotic medicines with them. The medicines were started, and they worked. Araceli began to eat. She stopped banging her head on the wall. She put on clothing. She began to talk. The church made a commitment that she would never run out of the drug.

I have before and after pictures of Araceli. Even though I know it is the same person, I wonder when I look at the change. I have a picture taken several years later, which shows a quiet woman standing beside one of the Sunday school children she now teaches.

She is a modern-day Mary Magdalene: a woman possessed of a demon

that surely would have killed her had not the
Lord intervened.

Jesus Healed Mental Illnesses

The nomenclature of the Bible doesn't allow
us to accurately compare apples to apples on
all of the diseases that Jesus healed. This passage from the King James translation gives
you an idea of this language challenge: "And
his fame went throughout all Syria: and they
brought unto him all sick people that were
taken with divers diseases and torments, and
those which were possessed with devils, and
those which were lunatick, and those that had
the palsy; and he healed them" (Matthew 4:24, KJV).[4]

> *People with physical diseases and diseases of the mind should be supported. To treat both equally would be to follow the example set by Christ.*

One thing we see for certain in all four Gospels is that Jesus didn't shy
away from any disease. I see zero evidence of him making any distinction
between those with purely physical diseases and those with neurological
and mental disorders.

Consider the reaction of the church today when someone has a physical illness versus a mental illness. If someone in the church gets a new
diagnosis of cancer, the disease is announced from the pulpit, prayers are
offered, meals are planned, and rides to the doctor are arranged. But if
someone gets a new diagnosis of depression or bipolar disorder, nothing
is said to the congregation. I find this interesting because while there are
numerous cases of mental disease in the Bible, there's not one clear case of
cancer. In no way am I suggesting that the response of churches to cancer
is at all wrong. People with physical diseases should be supported, just as
those with diseases of the mind should be. To treat both equally would be
to follow the example set by Christ.

Nowhere is mental disease better personified than when Jesus casts out
the demons from a mentally ill man of Gerasenes:

They arrived in the region of the Gerasenes, across the lake from Galilee. As Jesus was climbing out of the boat, a man who was possessed by demons came out to meet him. For a long time he had been homeless and naked, living in the tombs outside the town.

As soon as he saw Jesus, he shrieked and fell down in front of him. Then he screamed, "Why are you interfering with me, Jesus, Son of the Most High God? Please, I beg you, don't torture me!" For Jesus had already commanded the evil spirit to come out of him. This spirit had often taken control of the man. Even when he was placed under guard and put in chains and shackles, he simply broke them and rushed out into the wilderness, completely under the demon's power.

Jesus demanded, "What is your name?"

"Legion," he replied, for he was filled with many demons. The demons kept begging Jesus not to send them into the bottomless pit.

There happened to be a large herd of pigs feeding on the hillside nearby, and the demons begged him to let them enter into the pigs.

So Jesus gave them permission. Then the demons came out of the man and entered the pigs, and the entire herd plunged down the steep hillside into the lake and drowned.

LUKE 8:26-33

I want you to note one detail about Jesus healing this man. Look carefully at what happened when the demons went into a herd of swine. What did the swine do? They ran off a cliff and drowned in the lake. The swine did what animals never do. They killed themselves. They committed suicide.

Like our illustration of Araceli, the Bible includes an "after" portrait of the man healed by the Lord: "He was sitting at Jesus' feet, fully clothed and perfectly sane" (Luke 8:35).

These two stories—one modern, one ancient—illustrate that mental illness, like physical illness, is complicated, and many factors can affect the severity, diagnosis, and treatment of the illness. What we do know is that we are to treat those who have mental illnesses with the love and compassion of Christ.

These stories also shed light on our question of suicide. Is suicide a result of physical, mental, societal, or spiritual illness? The answer is yes, and we need to consider tools from all these arenas to help those we love.

Jesus Is Always for Life and against Death

Although the New Testament contains a number of those who suffered from mental illness, we don't have an example of someone who is suicidal in Jesus' presence. But suicide is a form of death, and the New Testament gives us a great deal of information about what Jesus thinks about death in general. We learn this from the tenor of all the Gospels, but it is highlighted in the Gospel of John.

In the eleventh chapter we learn that Lazarus, the brother of Mary and Martha, has taken ill. His sisters urge Jesus to come and visit him. But Jesus doesn't go immediately. When at last he travels to their home, Lazarus is already dead. In fact, Lazarus has been buried in a tomb for four days.

This is the place in the Bible where we get the beautiful lines of reassurance from Jesus about death, resurrection, and eternal life. Jesus says, "I am the resurrection and the life. Whoever believes in me, though he die, yet shall he live, and everyone who lives and believes in me shall never die" (John 11:25-26, ESV).

Jesus knows that he has the power to bring Lazarus back to life. Further, Jesus knows that his own death on the cross will make eternal life possible for *all* who believe in him. Yet when Jesus confronts the grief of those who love and mourn Lazarus, the Bible says, "Jesus wept" (John 11:35). This is the shortest and most poignant sentence in the Bible. It sums up Christ's feelings about death. He hates death so much that he is willing to die to put an end to it. He hates death so much that even though he will bring his friend back to life, he still cries at his passing.

Left to ourselves, we often don't know what to do about death. We don't know whether to bury the dead, burn the dead, or eat the dead. We don't know whether to cry for the dead or have a party. All of these have been acceptable at various times in history. How are we to view death? Without a clear authority on the subject, we're left with speculation. I believe that the Bible is that authority, and without the Bible,

Jesus taught us what we should think of death. We should cry when we lose someone. We may see them in heaven, but death still stinks.

we have no clear measure of what is right and wrong in life or in death.

Not long ago one of the nation's top newspapers ran a story about a woman holding a funeral for herself. One of the rules she imposed was that no attendee was allowed to cry. At the culmination of the funeral—she called it a life send-off party—she committed suicide.

Jesus taught us what we should think of death. We should cry when we lose someone. We may see them in heaven, but death still stinks.

Jesus had the power from God to raise the dead in Lazarus's time, and he still has the power to raise the dead today. He also has the power (and the desire) to bring those who are in despair back to hope. Jesus is and has always been for life.

Jesus demonstrates his unique identity as God through his power to raise the dead. In the Gospel of John, Jesus says, "Just as the Father gives life to those he raises from the dead, so the Son gives life to anyone he wants." In addition, Jesus uniquely claims to be the judge of the world: "The Father judges no one. Instead, he has given the Son absolute authority to judge" (John 5:21-22). Jesus gave his life to save the world, loved and healed those who suffered from illness, raised the dead (while still weeping at the death of his friend), and is ultimately in charge of judging the world. How does this shed light on our discussion of suicide?

IS SUICIDE AN UNFORGIVABLE SIN?

Through my speaking on suicide and interacting with people, I am often asked something like "Is suicide an unforgivable sin?" or "Is the person I love who committed suicide in heaven?" And I have to answer, "I don't know." While I believe that many who commit suicide are not in their right mind (and thus, I believe, less culpable), only God knows the state of our souls. And as I said above, it is for Christ to judge, not me.

For almost two thousand years in Western society, the church was the primary institution charged with preventing suicide. Only during the last century has this task fallen to other institutions. In point of fact, those other institutions may not be doing as effective a job as the church did, and the church had no medicines to offer.

The church *did* (and does), however, offer perspective on the afterlife, and what we think about the afterlife has a great deal to do with what we think about this life, including suicide. In recent years, an attitude of triviality has crept into our modern minds concerning the afterlife and judgment, and I think that has colored our discussions of suicide. In the past, the Roman Catholic Church has pronounced suicide an unforgivable sin. The reasoning was that a person must confess their sins in order for those sins to be forgiven. The sixth commandment tells us not to kill. The commandment could just as easily say, "Thou shall not kill *thyself*." Most would agree that in the scheme of things, murder is serious business. To murder oneself, therefore, is a sin. And by definition, one cannot confess this sin. Yet more than one suicide note includes the phrase, "God, forgive me."

While this has been the traditional view, I do not think that I can speak for the Lord here. *All* of us must throw ourselves on the mercy of Christ at Judgment Day, and I suspect that even popes and saints have a sin or two they forgot to mention in the confessional. Does that mean that none of us will get into heaven? Peter, quoting Proverbs, tells us that the just are "barely saved" (1 Peter 4:18). What about those who have killed themselves?

I believe that there is hope for those who have committed suicide and who had placed their trust in Jesus. That being said, the Bible holds out little or no hope for those who knew of Christ and rejected him in this life—regardless of how they exited the planet.

As we consider the question of "Is suicide an unforgivable sin?" I think it is wise to be prudent. Jesus is merciful, but suicide *is* a sin. It is disobeying God (who is for life), and it harms others, perhaps for generations. It is an act from which there is no turning back. If someone you know is contemplating suicide and is concerned about judgment, they should be. Life and death is not a game. It is a matter of life and death.

Nevertheless, for those who place their faith in Christ, I end this chapter with reassurance from Paul's letter to the Romans:

> I am convinced that nothing can ever separate us from God's love. Neither death nor life, neither angels nor demons, neither our fears for today nor our worries about tomorrow—not even the powers of hell can separate us from God's love. No power in the sky above or in the earth below—indeed, nothing in all creation will ever be able to separate us from the love of God that is revealed in Christ Jesus our Lord.
>
> ROMANS 8:38-39

As those Christian inmates in the high security prison demonstrated to me, nothing—not even a life sentence, not even an earthquake, not even a jailer saying he wants to die—can separate us from the love of God if we give ourselves to Christ. And that is cause for hope.

CHAPTER 7

Drugs and Alcohol

CATALYSTS FOR DEATH

※

Happy is the land whose king is a noble leader
and whose leaders feast at the proper time
to gain strength for their work, not to get drunk.

ECCLESIASTES 10:17

BEFORE WE CONCLUDE this section on a biblical worldview of suicide, I'd like to consider the topic of drugs and alcohol. Alcohol and drug dependence are associated with 10 to 15 percent higher suicide rates than in nondependent persons. Additionally, some 50 to 70 percent of those who commit suicide have drugs or alcohol in their system. Alcohol can rewire the brain, leaving behind a change that persists for years. Let me illustrate with examples from the real world by comparing and contrasting two patients.

I met the first patient when I was a resident moonlighting in my third year of residency. I used to drive two and a half hours to work a twenty-four-hour Saturday or Sunday shift at the small rural hospital, and I loved it. I loved the patients. I loved the nurses. I loved the doctors who worked there. Sometimes I'd see no more than a dozen patients a shift. Many nights I would sleep in the call room—dozing for dollars. But when I did have a patient, I was all on my own, the only doctor in the hospital.

One Saturday, just before midnight, the ER nurse woke me to say that the rescue squad was bringing in an unconscious sixteen-year-old female. I remember that she was sixteen because it was her birthday, a day I suspect she will never forget.

Her friends thought it would be a good idea to celebrate the milestone by introducing her to alcohol, and so they did. She'd never had a drink before. They drank, and they drank some more. She had to be home by ten, so they dropped her off in front of her house just before curfew. Her parents were out for the evening, but they'd left the front door open and the light on. As her friends drove off, she waved and started toward the front door, but she never made it. She got too tired, and she lay down on the autumn leaves to rest for a moment. Then she fell asleep, or rather, she fell into a stupor. When her parents arrived home just before midnight, they found her unconscious and unresponsive in the frost-covered leaves wearing jeans, a T-shirt, and a light sweater.

She was completely obtunded (Glasgow Coma score 3), with a core temperature of 93 degrees Fahrenheit, with shallow intermittent respirations and a blood pressure of 50/30. I intubated her and got no breath sounds on the left. The nurses could get no IV access. At that time, the ATLS (Advanced Trauma Life Support) protocol called for a cutdown if no peripheral IV access could be obtained. I called for backup, but the on-call doctor couldn't be located.

At times like this, it pays to follow the ABCs and stick to the protocols. I did a cutdown on the saphenous vein. (Thank you, Doctor Snell, from all of us you trained at Harvard and George Washington. We can still hear your British accent telling us that the saphenous vein runs "in front of, I said in front of, the medial malleolus.")

I got the line in her saphenous vein (yes!), and we ran 200cc of warmed fluid in, and then . . . the line stopped working. The chest X-ray came back, and—I don't know how—she'd dropped her left lung. Things were not looking good.

I needed IV access and fast or she was going to die. This was in the days before handheld ultrasounds. Getting a central line in her was going to be a challenge. She was cold, clamped down, short, already had one lung collapsed, and weighed in on the other side of pleasingly plump. A blood alcohol level came back. It was 0.14 percent, which is just below the level of intoxication in most states. I decided to put a central line in her femoral vein. (Thanks again, Dr. Snell, for the mnemonic NAVEL—Nerve, Artery, Vein, Empty Space, Lymphatic.) It worked! We started dumping warmed fluid into her.

Next, I got a chest tube in. Her pulse and blood pressure came back up to the "I wanna live" range. Her oxygen saturation level rose into the land of sunshine. Then I heard the sweetest sound a lone physician in a setting like that can hear—the chopping of the medical evacuation helicopter I'd called for!

The second patient was a man that came into another small hospital where I was moonlighting. By this time, I'd had more experience. I'd seen thousands more patients. Again, I was isolated. First, because I was in a small hospital on the Maine coast. Second, because it was nighttime and we were experiencing a severe snowstorm—a "Nor'easter." Lastly, because power lines were down, the hospital was running on a generator, and the CAT scanner couldn't be used.

A man was brought in by ambulance. He'd fallen walking up a slick, steep drive and landed on his face, which was a mess. Blood was everywhere. His eyes were swollen shut with lacerations. His nose was broken. His lips were swollen and cut. Blood soaked his thick, tangled beard. He was mumbling and not completely coherent. To me, he smelled like blood and booze.

His wife and sister came in with him. They insisted that he'd had nothing to drink. "Does he ever drink?" I asked. "No." They were adamant. He'd been a heavy drinker in his past, but he'd been sober for seven years. They told me that he'd been fixing up a cabin nearby. They hadn't seen him for three days. Apparently, he'd driven home in the snow and fallen while walking up the drive to his house.

He was a mess. His vital signs were normal other than his pulse, which was elevated at 120 BPM. Even as we examined him, he seemed to become more coherent. We drew labs. The lab tech told me that the blood alcohol level was going to take longer than his other labs. His blood alcohol level was the lab of greatest interest to me. If his mental status was caused by a high alcohol level, I could chance waiting for him to sober up. Even if it was high, he might have damaged his brain in the fall, but to me, he seemed drunk, not brain damaged. The safest thing to do would be to have a look at his brain with a CAT scanner. But to transfer him to a larger hospital two hours away in the middle of a blizzard was to put him, the rescue squad, and anyone else traveling on the road in increased danger.

One study suggests that 50 to 70 percent of those who commit suicide have alcohol or drugs in their systems.

I pressed the wife and sister again. Both said that he was a model AA attender. Both insisted he was sober. I decided to wait for the blood alcohol level anyway. An hour later we got it back. It showed a level of 0.512 percent.

His wife and sister kept asking what a level of 0.512 percent meant. (0.15 to 0.18 percent is intoxicated in most states.) I tried to explain, even writing down the percentage of blood to molecules of alcohol. My math explanations weren't working for them. They kept asking what it meant. Finally, I asked, "Have you ever heard of people who spontaneously catch on fire because they've had too much to drink?" A light went on in their eyes and they nodded in unison. "Don't light a match anywhere near him," I said. They nodded, for once satisfied with a straightforward explanation.

I watched this gentleman all night in the ER, and he improved by the hour. In the morning I sewed his face back together. As we talked, he told me that he'd been sober for seven years and hadn't had a single drink until he started just three days before. He apologized for causing any trouble. Late in the morning, his AA sponsor came in a four-wheel drive vehicle and took him home.

Here is my point in telling you of these two patients. The man who used to drink all the time but hadn't had a drink in seven years came into the ER with a blood alcohol level three to four times what stopped a new drinker from breathing. His level when I sent him home was higher than what the sweet sixteen gal came in with, and she was unable to breathe for herself. His brain had been permanently changed to accommodate an alcohol level that would kill another. The moral of the story is this: alcohol affects us long after we've had a drink.

These stories are germane to our discussion because alcohol and depression are a lethal combination. One study suggests that 50 to 70 percent of those who commit suicide have alcohol or drugs in their systems. Although there are medicines to help those withdrawing from the chronic use of alcohol, and there are drugs that make drinking alcohol unpleasant (such as Antabuse), there are still no medicines that actually treat alcoholism, just as there are currently no medicines that can reverse the acute effects of alcohol. The most effective treatment for alcohol addiction is still, by and large, spiritual. Twelve-step programs have proven to be the most effective way to treat alcoholism. In fact, treatment wise, not much has changed regarding alcohol addiction since the Bible was written, and the Bible has a surprising amount to say on the subject. So let's open a Bible and see what we can learn and then consider the implications for our conversation about suicide.

ALCOHOL IN THE OLD TESTAMENT

Where does alcohol first show up in the Bible? The first instance is purely conjecture. If you ask the average person what Eve and Adam ate (that they shouldn't have) in the Garden of Eden, they would likely tell you that Eve plucked an apple from the tree of the knowledge of good and evil. In fact, there is no apple tree mentioned in this portion of the Bible. Why all the paintings of Eve holding an apple, then? It probably comes from St. Jerome's Vulgate translation of the Bible into Latin (around AD 400), where the word for evil and apple (*malum*) is the same.

Rabbis of old used to speculate instead that what Adam and Eve ate was the "fruit of the vine," or alcohol. As we skip through the rest of Scripture, we'll see why that wasn't such a far-fetched speculation. In fact, the reasons Eve was tempted are the same as the reasons so many of us are first tempted to try alcohol. Eve tried the fruit because it tasted good, because it looked good (think of all those ads with liquor swirling in the light surrounded by gleaming crystal glasses), and because it made people think they were wise. Indeed, most drinkers I've met believe they've picked up additional IQ points once they've had a few.

We do not know if the fruit Adam and Eve ate was the fruit of the vine, but they certainly acted like it. They seem to have woken up afterward—ashamed, remorseful, hiding, lying, and making excuses for what they had done.

The next alcohol incident in the Bible (only a few pages later) is *not* conjecture.[1] It occurs after Noah and his family dock their boat on *terra firma*. Noah takes up farming, grows grapes, and makes wine. Then one day Noah gets drunk and passes out while naked. Noah's son, Ham, in some way molests or humiliates him while he is drunk. Here the Bible gives us our first explicit warning about losing control of ourselves by drinking: Don't get drunk. Don't get drunk around strangers. Don't get drunk around someone like Ham. You won't know if you have a Ham lurking as your date, your friend, or your family member until you get drunk—so don't get drunk.

For a number of years, I practiced medicine next to a military facility *and* a college. I cannot tell you how much misery could be prevented if parents taught their children—and their children heeded!—the Bible's first lesson about drinking.

The example of Noah seems to typify a pattern of God hitting the reset button with the human race and us blowing it with a bottle of bourbon in our hand. The next instance takes place after God hits the reset button and destroys the wicked cities of Sodom and Gomorrah.[2] These were cities that gave themselves over to sensual pleasures. Honor, truth, and virtue were no longer valued. Hospitality and the sheltering of strangers were no longer practiced. Rather, sexual perversion and drunkenness were the norm in Sodom.

Lot, his wife, and his two daughters were led out of Sodom just before God rained fire down on the cities in judgment. But Lot's wife longed for her old life in Sodom. Alas, the Lord let her join it, and she became a pillar of salt. From this point onward in the Scriptures, Sodom is the archetype of a wicked place. When Jesus mentions Sodom, he would have us understand that everything it stood for is condemned. Even though Lot and his two daughters escaped Sodom, the ways of the place clung to them.

Lot and his daughters fled to an isolated cave in the hills. The daughters, believing that they would never encounter other people, decided to conceive children by their father. They got their father drunk and slept with him. Both conceived. Alcohol may not have been the sole cause of their problems, but it certainly didn't help. Lot forgot the first rule of drinking in the Bible.

As we proceed through the Bible, we come to an episode of drunken partying that many are familiar with. It took place when the Hebrews wandered in the wilderness and Moses went up Mount Sinai.[3] While Moses was talking with God, the partying began back at the base camp. The debauchery is portrayed in Cecil B. DeMille's *The Ten Commandments*. This makes for good cinema, but there is another, less titillating episode that occurs later in the Hebrews' wanderings, from which we can infer the destructive role of alcohol.

Aaron (Moses' brother) was high priest, and his sons assisted him in his duties. Two of his sons apparently got drunk and performed a ritual with incense and fire they were not supposed to. The Lord struck them dead in his anger. Directly after this, the Lord instituted this rule: "Drink no wine or strong drink, you or your sons with you, when you go into the tent of meeting, lest you die. It shall be a statute forever throughout your generations" (Leviticus 10:9, ESV). Similar to this was the institution of the Nazirite vow, taken by those who wanted to "[set] themselves apart to the

LORD in a special way" (Numbers 6:2). Those who took the vow were to eschew luxury, wine, and strong drink and anything that could be easily fermented, such as grapes and raisins, and they were to let their hair grow. What these passages illustrate is that "sober" was to be the watchword of the people on earth who represented God and heaven.

ESTHER, ALCOHOL, AND REDEMPTION

Scripture warns us repeatedly and consistently about the perils of drunkenness. Noah, Lot, Nadab and Abihu, Nabal, the Philistines and Samson, Absalom and Amnon, Elah, and many others all suffer from the consequences of excessive alcohol intake. However, nothing warns us like the biblical book of Esther.

Esther is a unique book in Scripture. Unlike other biblical books, Esther takes place entirely in the ancient world's epicenter of pagan culture, in the court of the Persian King Xerxes. God is never mentioned. Prayers are never made. The characters in Esther live outside of God's will in the capital city of the Medo-Persian empire (in what is modern-day Iran).

Xerxes the Great ruled a kingdom divided into 127 provinces stretching from India through the Fertile Crescent and south to Ethiopia. Xerxes summoned the governors and their delegations from these provinces to the capital city of Susa. His goal was to impress attendees with his wealth. He threw a party for thousands lasting six months. Six months of feasting day and night. Six months of hosting 127 delegations. Six months of housing and feeding them *and* boarding their horses, camels, and other livestock. Six months of governors and court officials jockeying to see who could get nearest to Xerxes. Meanwhile, Xerxes was lobbying the governors of his empire to attack the Greek city-states with him. At last, the grand finale came—a week where all those living in and around the palace were invited to join in the festivities.

Xerxes decreed that the wine was to flow. "The bar is open! You don't have to drink, but if you do, drink all you want." And drink they did. They sat on sofas made of silver and gold with cushions of silk. They walked on floors with mosaics made from stones across the empire. They feasted and they feasted. They drank and they drank. They raised thousands of gold goblets captured from all over the known world. And then they got to bragging. Xerxes had many wives and concubines, but none was more beautiful than the queen, Vashti. Xerxes said there wasn't a woman alive who looked better. An idea worked its way into his alcohol-fogged brain. Why not show all these men Vashti's beauty?

Xerxes sent word to Vashti in the part of the palace where she and thousands of women were holding their own party: "Put your crown on, take everything else off, and come show my friends how ravishing you are." It seemed like such a good idea—until Vashti sent back a note flatly refusing his request.

Now the worst thing you can do with a tyrant, from one running an empire to one running your department at work, is to make them look bad in front of others. Xerxes was livid, and he was drunk.

Xerxes turned to his top advisers and asked them what they would do. One suggested that if the king let his wife get away with refusing his request, all the women in the kingdom would follow suit. So they made a law that all wives should obey their husbands, and Vashti should lose her position as queen and never see Xerxes again. In short order, Vashti was deposed.

A period of time passed. The reader can assume this is when Xerxes conducted his ill-fated campaign invading Greece. Eventually, Xerxes came back to the palace. He remembered his beautiful wife, and he missed her. But alas, a law of the land was a law of the land and could never be rescinded. Even the king couldn't undo his banishment of Vashti. The king's advisers came up with an idea. Forget Vashti! Why not hold a kingdom-wide beauty contest looking for the fairest virgin? The winner would become Xerxes's new queen.

This is the stuff of modern reality TV: people who have never met go through a series of interviews and engineered circumstances and then choose a spouse. The casting call went out, and the Miss Medo-Persian contest began.

In Susa, the palace city, there lived a Jewish man named Mordecai.

Many Jews lived in the city. They had been brought from Israel as captives more than a century before, but a decree by King Cyrus sixty years prior had allowed them to go home. Many, however, stayed. They preferred the lives they had established in Persia. Mordecai was one who stayed, and when he heard about the beauty contest, he thought of Esther, an orphaned cousin whom he had adopted and raised. Esther was a looker. She had style and grace. Surely she could win.

The contest set the empire ablaze with excitement, each province wanting to gain the power and access to the royal court that having a queen from their ranks would afford them. Esther, the girl next door, appeared before the screening judges and qualified with ease. The eunuch supervising the women in the contest was impressed by Esther too. He gave her seven servants and put her in the best apartment in the contestants' part of the palace.

Each contestant spent twelve months with personal trainers, dieticians, and beauty coaches. When their twelve-month preparation was up, it was their turn to appear before Xerxes. If they won, they'd be given the crown and all that went with it. If they lost, they'd be given a spot in the king's harem.

Esther, face shining, with only a hint of makeup, appeared before Xerxes. Xerxes was smitten. He placed the crown on her head. A party was thrown throughout the kingdom. They had a new queen! Esther must have mentioned her guardian, Mordecai, to her new husband, because Mordecai was appointed to a judgeship in Susa. Still, Esther, as per Mordecai's instructions, told no one that she was Jewish.

Now a side plot was also taking place during all of this. (This is the stuff of a high-budget miniseries.) Mordecai refused to bow to the king's grand vizier, Haman. Mordecai was a Jew, and Haman was from a people called the Amalekites. The Amalekites were an old foe of the Jews. Haman couldn't stand that a Jew wouldn't bow to him, so he plotted to kill not only Mordecai but every single Jew in the kingdom.

Haman convinced Xerxes that the Jews in his empire were troublemakers and that they should be exterminated. "I'll even put ten thousand talents of silver in the national treasury to make sure this gets done right,"

Haman promised. The king refused Haman's money but agreed to exterminate the Jews. To set the date for the holocaust, Haman threw dice, called purim. Anyone who killed a Jewish man, woman, or child could seize all their possessions.

And what did Haman and the king do after they hatched this plot? They sat down and got drunk, and the city's inhabitants wondered what was becoming of their society.[4]

The book of Esther is fueled by alcohol. Esther, Mordecai, and the Jewish people were in a rough spot. The kingdom's edicts could never be reversed. Esther rose to the occasion at considerable risk to her own life. The Jewish people throughout the kingdom were saved. I'll leave it to you to read the rest of the book to find out how she did it—or to wait until the high-budget miniseries is released.

To celebrate Esther's victory, Jews today celebrate the holiday of Purim annually. The book of Esther is read aloud, and every time Haman's name is mentioned, everyone yells, boos, stamps their feet, blows raspberries, and makes a ruckus. Baskets of wine, food, and treats are given to the poor and to family and friends. Adults are allowed, even encouraged, to drink too much. Despite this, it is also a time to recall that alcohol encourages people to make poor decisions. A decent person will do what they would otherwise refrain from when they are sober. But a less-than-decent person will do things a normal person wouldn't consider even when they are plastered.

ALCOHOL IN THE NEW TESTAMENT

This is the tenor of the Old Testament concerning alcohol. So, are we to abstain completely from alcohol? Let us turn to the New Testament to see how the subject was dealt with when the Lord walked the earth in flesh. Specifically, let us turn to Jesus' first miracle as it is recorded at the beginning of John's Gospel.[5]

Alcohol encourages people to make poor decisions.

Jesus and his disciples have been invited to a wedding in Cana. Mary, Jesus' mother, is also present. The wedding appears to be well under way, and the hosts have run out of wine. How did they run short? Perhaps it was poor planning. Perhaps the wedding party didn't have enough money. Maybe it was because Jesus showed up with a dozen men that drank, well, like sailors. Regardless of the cause, Mary appeals to her son Jesus to fix the situation. Jesus answers in what appears to be a somewhat snippy manner. He begs off, claiming that it isn't time yet for him to be doing miracles.

Now there is no place in the Bible that rings truer than this scene, if one has witnessed a Jewish mother bring up a whiz kid—and I have. My wife was raised Jewish and became a Christian shortly after I did. Since Judaism runs through the mother, technically both of our children are Jewish. Over the years, many times I've heard my wife ask her son to do a favor for her. I've seen him balk and get a little snippy. Yet without fail he sets aside whatever he is doing and fulfills her request. Apparently, it's an ancient Jewish mother–oldest son thing.

And so, Jesus has the servants at the wedding fill six large barrels with water, and the water becomes wine. When the wine is presented to the best man and he tastes it, he exclaims, "This is fantastic wine! I can't believe it! Where did this come from? Usually a wedding party will serve the good stuff first and then when everybody is buzzed and can't tell the difference, they'll bring out the cheap wine. But you've saved the best for last!"[6]

Like virtually everything around Jesus, there are many layers to this story. First, he is still his mother's son, honoring the fifth commandment. Second, he is revealing God's approval for the institution of marriage. Third, the wine is an analogy for Christ himself. The best has been saved for last. Fourth, at the time of Jesus, the most worshiped god in the pagan pantheon was Bacchus (his Roman name; Dionysus is his Greek name). Bacchus had to be taught how to ferment wine, but here Jesus shows himself the master of all creation—including the fermentation process.[7]

Certainly, Jesus would not have made water into wine if he didn't want us to drink. Christianity is not the religion of teetotalers. In fact, Jesus' critics accused him of drinking and having too good a time at parties.[8] But then again, Jesus didn't come to remove any of the wisdom from the Old Testament, and the Old Testament unremittingly reminds us to be moderate in our consumption of alcohol.

One of the most important holy days in the Jewish calendar is a remembrance of the Jews being saved. I'm not talking about Purim but the celebration of Passover. This is a meal in which the Jews commemorate being rescued from slavery in Egypt and being passed over by the angel of death, which had come to slay all the firstborn sons living in Egypt. On the original Passover, families were to sacrifice a Passover lamb; spread the Passover lamb's blood on the wooden lintel, pillar, and post of their entrance door; and eat the Passover lamb. If they did this, the blood on the wooden doorway locked out the angel of death.

When Jesus celebrated this meal for the last time, he wished to show how all generations could now share in being "passed over" by death. Jesus was to be sacrificed on a cross so that we might live.

Jesus took a cup of wine and blessed it. He said it was his blood, the blood of the Passover lamb—the lamb that takes away the sins of the world. When his blood was spread on the wooden cross, the angel of death was defeated. The cross became a doorway to heaven standing open to all who would have eternal life. But in order to have that life, we must accept Jesus as our Passover lamb.

Of note, nowhere in the Old Testament description of Passover is wine explicitly mentioned. I don't think Jesus would raise the Passover wine to the level of meaning he did if he intended for us not to drink it. Indeed, when he was finished with the wine and bread at Passover, he promised to drink again with his followers once he was resurrected.[9]

Jesus was offered sour wine while he was dying on the cross. He sipped it and died.[10] The wine we will share with him in heaven will not be like that sour wine, but like the sublime wine served at the wedding at Cana—because it will be another wedding, the wedding of Christ with his bride, the church.

WHAT DOES THE BIBLE SAY ABOUT DRUGS?

So far, we've been discussing alcohol, but what does the Bible say about drugs? Drugs show up in Scripture in two ways: drugs alone and drugs mixed with alcohol. In both cases, the results are deadly.

One of the first examples of drugs in Scripture can be found in the book of Genesis. Then, as today, we see how drugs can have a powerful hold over those who crave them. In Genesis 30:14-18, we find the story of how one woman allows another to sleep with her husband so that she can obtain the drug she wants. (Both women were the man's wives, but there was a rivalry between them.) The son that results from this sex-for-drug trade is called Issachar, which means "hire" or "reward." In this instance, the drug is mandrake, which is derived from the mandrake root.[11]

Often alcohol is mentioned in the Bible along with "strong drinks." Strong drinks are not a reference to distilled liquor. Other than one freezing method used in ancient times to increase the alcohol content of wine, distillation of alcohol did not exist in biblical times. The "strong drink" refers to wine mixed with mandrake or other narcotic-type plants. This is the case with the wine mixed with myrrh, which Jesus refused on the cross.[12]

We get some indication of what God might think of the powerful drugs we have today from several references in the book of Revelation. For example, Revelation 22:14-15 says, "Blessed are those who wash their robes. They will be permitted to enter through the gates of the city and eat the fruit from the tree of life. Outside the city are the dogs—the sorcerers, the sexually immoral, the murderers, the idol worshipers, and all who love to live a lie." In this passage, John is describing those who may enter heaven and those who may not. Those who "wash their robes," which means those who keep God's commandments, may enter. But "sorcerers" are among those who may not. What does sorcery have to do with drugs? The Greek word translated here as "sorcerers" is *pharmakos*, from which we derive the modern word *pharmacy*. It refers, at least in part, to drugs. This and other passages seem to indicate that drugs have the power to bewitch us and cut us off from God.

Although drugs were potent in biblical times, the potency of modern synthetic drugs is astounding. The synthetic narcotic fentanyl is fifty times more potent than heroin. Carfentanil, a newer synthetic narcotic, is five thousand to ten thousand times more potent than heroin. To get that into perspective, a dose of Carfentanil smaller than a grain of sand is lethal. A one-kilogram (2.2-pound) shipment of Carfentanil mailed from China and intercepted by Canadian authorities contained enough of the drug to kill every person in Canada.

The potency of modern drugs is frightening. They are truly bioweapons. That is one reason the United States has seen overdose deaths go from five thousand in 1968 to over seventy thousand in 2017. This is nothing short of demonic. Today more than ever we would be wise to heed God's warnings about the power and lethality of drug addiction.

MODERATION AND RESTRAINT

We see in the letters from Paul and others that wine should be used in moderation and that those who can't moderate their drinking should not hold positions of authority in the church.[13] In reading the New Testament's instructions, the saying "moderation in all things" certainly comes to mind.

Some of us, however, must moderate more than others. For most people, small amounts of sugar are a treat. But to the diabetic, sugar can be deadly.

Likewise, wine and drink may be fine for some, but not for those suffering from depression and suicidal thoughts. All too often, alcohol and drugs weaken our impulse control with deadly results. The Bible may not prohibit imbibing alcohol, but it gives repeated warnings about using it to excess. If someone has a family history of suicide or alcoholism, perhaps they should put off having a drink until they can sit down with the one who made water into wine.

Modern drugs are truly bioweapons. That is one reason US overdose deaths have increased from 5,000 in 1968 to over 70,000 in 2017.

PART 3

How You Can Help

No man is an island, entire of itself;
every man is a piece of the continent,
a part of the main.
If a clod be washed away by the sea,
Europe is the less, as well as
if a promontory were,
as well as if a manor of thy friend's
or of thine own were:
any man's death diminishes me,
because I am involved in mankind,
and therefore never send to know
for whom the bell tolls;
it tolls for thee.

JOHN DONNE

CHAPTER 8

Talking to a Loved One

WE ARE OUR BROTHER'S (AND SISTER'S) KEEPERS

※

*It is easy to love the people far away. It is not always
easy to love those close to us. It is easier to give a cup of rice
to relieve hunger than to relieve the loneliness and pain of
someone unloved in our own home. Bring love into your home
for this is where our love for each other must start.*

MOTHER TERESA

WE'VE COME TO THE PART of this book where the rubber meets the road: how to approach someone who might be suicidal. Perhaps you are a concerned parent. A friend. A youth pastor. A church elder. A neighbor. A teacher. A sister, nephew, aunt, or son. It is almost certain that at some point in your life, someone you know will be thinking about suicide.

As an ER doctor, I rehearsed emergency scenarios. When a life-or-death situation presented, I knew the drill. I had done my thinking in advance. I was prepared to act.

Suicide is, by definition, an emergency. How you respond is a matter of life or death. The point of this chapter is not to make you a professional counselor. Rather, it is intended to help you

1. get your loved one help in an emergency, and
2. support your friend, colleague, student, or loved one through the healing process.

We will begin with questions—first for yourself and then for your loved one. If your loved one is in immediate danger, this section will help you know what to do. If your loved one is not in immediate danger, you will learn ways to offer support and hope. The last part of the chapter focuses on a specific tool to help you

1. understand factors that may be contributing to your loved one's depression, and
2. identify resiliency-building behaviors to help your loved one heal.

QUESTIONS TO ASK YOURSELF BEFORE APPROACHING A LOVED ONE

Suicide is a challenging subject, often shrouded in darkness. It is important to shine a light on your own experiences, memories, and feelings. So before approaching a loved one, ask yourself a few pointed questions, and answer them honestly.

Am I Clear about My Beliefs on Suicide?

Throughout this book, I have presented a biblical worldview: God is for life. Satan is against life. Jesus puts it like this: "The thief [Satan] comes only to steal and kill and destroy. I came that they may have life and have it abundantly" (John 10:10, ESV). Jesus gave his life not so that people can kill themselves but so that they can have abundant life. If someone is thinking about suicide, they are being deceived by the author of lies rather than listening to the God of truth. As a Christian, your job is to compassionately and lovingly shine a light into the darkness. The source of this light is Jesus, as revealed through the Bible.

We are indeed our brother's and sister's keepers. We have a responsibility for the welfare of others.

We've all met teachers who don't like students, doctors without compassion, and preachers without love. The last thing a person who is suicidal needs is someone trying to help them who is conflicted about what they are doing. So let's be clear: from a biblical worldview, suicide is wrong. The Ten Commandments forbid murder. God never wants one of his beloved children to kill themselves. Before you can convince someone else of this truth, you need to be certain of it yourself.

What Do I Feel When I Think about a Person I Know Who Committed Suicide?

Recall the first suicide you knew of personally. How close were you to the person? What events and conversations led up to the suicide? Do you feel any responsibility? Guilt? Regrets? Do you believe that you could have done something more to intercede?

If you have multiple experiences with suicide, in what ways were the circumstances and emotions you experienced similar? In what ways were they different? Have you processed your sadness, frustration, and anger? Before approaching someone who might be suicidal, it's a good idea to write down your experiences with suicide and discuss them with others.

Is It My Business to Get Involved in Someone Else's Life-and-Death Decisions?

Biblically, we learn the answer to this question by looking at the Bible's first murder: Cain killing his little brother, Abel. When God asked Cain where his brother Abel was, Cain infamously quipped, "Am I my brother's keeper?" The lesson of the story is that we are indeed our brother's and sister's keepers. We have a responsibility for the welfare of others.

How far does the Bible take this obligation? It gives us responsibility for our brother or sister, for someone in our church, for someone at work, and even for our enemy. Biblically speaking, our obligation to others extends so far that if our enemy's donkey stumbles under a heavy load, we're required by the law of God to help.[1]

In our hyperindividualistic culture, we can always find excuses for not getting involved. From a biblical worldview, however, it's not okay to wait until it's too late.

QUESTIONS TO ASK TO DETERMINE IF SOMEONE IS IN IMMEDIATE DANGER

If you think someone might be suicidal and you've taken your own pulse on the subject, what do you do next? Below are three questions that will help clarify the best course of action.

I've Noticed You've Seemed Distracted Lately— Can You Share What's Going On?

If possible, pick a safe, quiet place to approach your loved one. Don't charge up while they are standing at a cash register and ask, "Are you thinking about killing yourself?" Instead, sit down to coffee and begin with something like this: "Courtney, I've noticed that you seem pre-occupied lately (or a little distracted, sad, different, down). Can you share what's going on?" If Courtney answers, "I'm fine," you might follow up with, "Yes, but how are you doing, *really*?"

In my experience, if you care deeply about a person, they'll open up. Throughout my time in clinical medicine, I was never sued or named in a suit for malpractice. Partly, I was lucky. But another reason was that I kept in mind that even though the patients I was caring for didn't necessarily understand the science behind what I was doing, everybody has a PhD in detecting attitude. They know whether you care.

If the person begins to cry, let them. Resist the temptation to hush them or tell them that everything is going to be okay. If they are thinking about suicide, things are not "okay." Be prepared to listen quietly. Bring a handkerchief and hand it to them, and make sure you have one for yourself, too. You want to know how they are really doing.

Remember, this isn't about you or your comfort level; it is about them. We live in a world of shallowness and pretense. We're forever saying, "Have a nice one" and smiling for selfies while the truth remains hidden inside.

When history looks back on our generation, they'll marvel that we were the generation that smiled for a photo right before we jumped off the bridge. It's time to get real.

Have You Thought about Hurting Yourself?

When it comes to communicating and asking very hard things, I've found it helpful to have a script memorized that I don't vary from. Having a script doesn't mean you care any less; it means you care enough to be prepared. Every single time I have to tell someone that they've lost a loved one, I begin by saying, "I have some bad news I have to tell you," and then I go on to tell them that their loved one has died.

My scripted question for suicide is "Have you thought about hurting yourself?" At some level, every person knows that committing suicide is wrong. I think that most want to be asked whether they are thinking about it. They want to share the burden. Most want to be stopped.

Do You Have a Plan?

You'd be surprised how forthcoming folks are when you ask about their thoughts on suicide. If someone says they have considered suicide, ask if they have a plan. If they have a plan and the means to carry it through, you must act immediately. This is the time to call 911 and say that you are sitting with someone who is suicidal and has a plan. If it's appropriate, and you are certain that you and they will be safe, you can take them to the emergency department yourself.

At some point, a suicidal person may balk and say something like "I don't have insurance" or "I need to see about my dog first." I would gently dismiss these excuses. You wouldn't walk away from someone clutching their chest in pain if they gave you an excuse.

Never agree to keep someone's suicide plans secret. Suicide is still viewed by society as murder, and you would never keep secret someone's plans to murder someone. Getting a person help is the beginning of their road back to life and recovery.

If someone flat out lies to you and denies that they are suicidal, and in fact they are not telling the truth, morally and legally, you're not responsible. Even in the ER, the staff works under the assumption and expectation of honesty on the part of a patient.

This is an uncomfortable subject, but when asking about a plan, you need to also ask about the means of committing suicide. If someone's plan is to shoot themselves, get the firearms out of their house. If they plan to overdose, get rid of the pills, leaving them only a day or two's supply of those medicines they must take. You would be surprised how many people—even trained professionals—forget this step. Ask how they plan to kill themselves, and then as soon as possible remove the means to do so.

CONTINUING THE CONVERSATION

If the situation does not require you to call 911 or take the person immediately to an ER, then continue the conversation. Getting a fuller picture of the situation will help you assess how to help and who to call. Below are some examples of how to continue the conversation.

Tell Me about Any Experiences with Suicide You've Had in Your Family or with Friends.

One of the best predictors of the future is the past. If your loved one denies feeling suicidal and there appears to be no immediate emergency, you should take time to question them about any personal history with suicide. Is there a suicide attempt in their past? Do they have a family history of suicide? Did someone they know commit suicide? How recent was it? Have they just gone through a major life stressor like a divorce, breakup, job loss, or loss of a loved one? Have they just gotten a serious medical diagnosis?

When I say "serious medical diagnosis," I have a caveat. The seriousness of the diagnosis can be subjective. What may seem trivial to you or me may not be to them because of a difference in age, experience, personality, or character. I once saw a fifteen-year-old girl in the ER for a sprained ankle. She became distraught because she couldn't compete in a high school track meet. Compared to the other patients I was caring for at the time, she had the most minor injury. But she returned to the ER within twenty-four hours, suicidal. She had not been depressed or had any previous complaints of suicidal ideation, but in her reckoning, not being in the high school track meet was cause for ending her life.

Bottom line: a past history helps you assess the risk factors that predispose someone to suicide.

Are You Taking Drugs or Drinking?

Remember that drugs and alcohol are accelerants to suicide. In fact, the vast majority of the suicidal patients I saw in the ER had drugs or alcohol in their system when they tried to kill themselves. So please don't forget to ask your loved one if they are using drugs or alcohol.

Parents who ask their children—even adult children—about drug and alcohol use may not get a straight answer. Nonetheless, *someone* must ask, preferably as nonjudgmentally as possible. This is not to say that the one asking must have no opinions about drugs and alcohol. The point is to get a fuller picture of reality so you know what you are dealing with. Your goal is for them to refrain from using alcohol and drugs while they are depressed and to seek help with quitting if they can't stop.

Again, an example: smoking is bad for you. All doctors and nurses should urge their patients to quit. But the object is not just to check off a box on the health care provider's to-do list; it's for the patient to quit and to sustain the new behavior.

I used to work with a doctor who took it personally when a patient smoked. He would bully his patients to stop by telling them the scary facts about smoking (as if they didn't know). We arranged a bet about who could get the most people to quit smoking over the next six months.

If a smoker came to the ER with a complaint of a cough, I wouldn't even ask if they smoked. (You can tell by smell.) I'd send them for a chest X-ray. When I put the chest X-ray up on the screen, I'd stare at it to make sure nothing bad was going on, and then I'd whistle and say, "Looks like Marlboro country. Any chance you're a smoker?" When they nodded yes, I'd say, "Wow, it's hard to quit, isn't it?" Then we'd have a talk about how difficult it is to quit. I'd share what had worked for others, and I kept brochures on quitting handy.

Guess who won the bet?

One of the best ways to help someone struggling with alcohol or drug dependency is to introduce them to someone who has struggled with a similar addiction and overcome it. You can find that person in nearly every church, and they can take your loved one to their first AA, NA, or Celebrate Recovery meeting.

If You Do Become Suicidal, Do You Know What to Do?
If the person you are concerned about has no suicidal plans or thoughts but they are depressed, it's a good idea to bring up what they should do if they become suicidal. This is similar to the situation of evaluating someone in the ER for chest pain. If I determined that their chest pain wasn't a heart attack or other serious malady, nonetheless I'd give them a list of warning signs and instructions on when to return.

None of us is perfect. We all make mistakes. Situations change. Leave the door open for someone to get back to you or someone else if they do become suicidal. Make sure that they have a number to call, and that it is written down—whether it is as simple as writing down 911 or the National Suicide Prevention Lifeline, 1-800-273-TALK (8255). You can also text the Lifeline number to them so they have it in their phone.

TWO CATEGORIES OF DEPRESSION
As we continue to ask our loved one about their depression, I want to point out that mental health workers used to divide major depressive episodes into two categories: endogenous (depression coming from unknown causes and thought to be based solely on our genetics and biology) and exogenous (depression that started from factors outside

ourselves, such as the loss of a loved one, job, health, etc., also known as reactive depression).

Therapists, psychologists, psychiatrists, and family doctors made this distinction because of the understanding that exogenous depression could be influenced by and was partly under the control of the patient. The depression had a definable cause. Let me give you an example. It stands to reason that if someone develops depression after losing a job, the depression might be resolved by searching for and landing a new job. Defining a depression as an exogenous or endogenous case sometimes placed responsibility on the patient, but it also gave them control. However, this way of looking at the origins of depression has largely been abandoned by the mental health community over the last thirty years.

Abandoning this way of approaching depression was, however, primarily done for expedience, not clinical experience. We live in a world that values immediate answers, cure-alls, and magic bullets. We've come to believe that a pill can fix everything instantly—and sometimes it can. But what this approach leaves out is the long-term spiritual consequences of our actions.

Consider this illustration. A century ago, if someone contracted a venereal disease, they were in real trouble. For the most part, they were stuck with it. Modern antibiotics have substantially made such serious consequences a thing of the past. Obviously, that's a good thing. But while the physical consequences of freewheeling sexual lifestyles may no longer leave us with syphilitic brains, the spiritual and psychological consequences have left us with a divorce rate unimaginable by our grandparents and with the primary unit of society, the family, in shambles.

Antidepressants have helped millions of people, so I am *not* suggesting that antidepressants are unnecessary—and neither should you. Never encourage a person to stop a prescription medicine without the knowledge and consent of the prescriber.

Yet it's an established fact that the sale of antidepressants is a multibillion-dollar industry. There has been a great push by the manufacturers of antidepressants to put people on them and to keep them on them indefinitely. Thus, whether your loved one is currently taking antidepressants or not, I'd advise patients, therapists, and friends of the depressed to expend whatever time is needed to get to the bottom of a definable cause of depression—if one can be found—and, if possible, to address the cause.

SIG E CAPS: SCREENING FOR CAUSES AND WAYS TO HELP

As we discussed in chapter 4, SIG E CAPS (sleep, interest, guilt, energy, concentration, appetite, psychomotor, and suicidal ideation) is a time-tested tool used by professionals to screen for depression. In addition to screening for whether someone is depressed, I propose using SIG E CAPS to look for causes as well as ways we might help.

Think of it this way. Suppose one morning someone starts banging their head on the wall and develops a headache. They go to their doctor and complain of a headache, and their doctor writes a prescription for pain medication. Even if the pills relieve the headache, wouldn't it be better to find the cause?

Likewise, I think more time should be spent understanding the causes of the depression. Sadness and depression may indeed be the result solely of chemical imbalances. Antidepressants can be a wonderful treatment. But many depressions—ones that involve chemical imbalances and ones that don't—are the symptoms of deeper causes. You'll never know if you don't go searching.

Let's get back to our friend Courtney. Let's suppose that you have Courtney's trust and that you sense she may be depressed. Let's go through a script of how that conversation could take place, now looking for causes and ways to help. We'll use SIG E CAPS as the framework.

Starting the Conversation

One way to begin is to simply ask, "Courtney, have you been feeling depressed (or blue or down) lately?" If her answer is yes, ask her to describe what she means by that. Follow-up questions can include these:

- How long have you been feeling this way?
- When did you first notice the change?
- Have you ever experienced this before?
- If so, what did you do to get better?

Questions like these will give you a clearer picture of the situation and clues about what to ask next.

One of the parameters for diagnosing a major depressive disorder is a depressed mood for two or more weeks. If your loved one has had a history of a major depression in the past that responded well to antidepressants, encourage them to see their doctor as soon as possible. A prescription for the medicine that worked last may be the next move.

Sleep (S of SIG E CAPS)

Another helpful question is "How have you been sleeping lately?" A key symptom of depression is early-morning awakening, where the person wakes between 2:00 and 4:00 a.m. and has trouble falling back to sleep. While a night or two of poor sleep is not something to worry about, chronic lack of sleep is never healthy—physically, emotionally, or spiritually. With depression, your loved one may either sleep a great deal more or a good deal less. It's important to take note of changes in either direction.

While trouble sleeping might be simply a sign of depression, you would be surprised how many people are put on sleep medications and antidepressants who are also drinking eight, nine, or ten cups of coffee a day. Likewise, I've met folks drinking two gallons of iced tea a day complaining of trouble sleeping. Difficulty sleeping can be a *symptom* of depression, but poor sleep hygiene can also be a *cause* of depression.

GOOD SLEEP HYGIENE: CURATING WHAT YOU POUR IN

If your loved one is experiencing sleep disturbances, you might want to ask a follow-up question such as this: "Do you have a television in the bedroom, or are you watching the TV or computer before going to bed?"

Watching anything right before bedtime is not considered good sleep hygiene—disturbing themes are even worse.

If your loved one went to a Greek or Egyptian physician 2,500 years ago and complained of melancholy, or depression, they might be asked questions such as these:

- What music have you been listening to?
- What poetry are you reading?
- Where are you going for your daily walk?

Looking for the link between depression and what we are putting into our brains is a time-honored tack that has only recently gone out of vogue. What we put into our brains impacts our sleep habits as well as our psyche.

I'm astounded at the number of dystopian offerings available on television and on streaming services. Vampires suck people's blood, mutants walk about killing people, zombies come up out of the lawn, aliens invade from outer space, and thugs empty round after round of bullets into the world. Stalkers stalk, serial killers go about their grisly business, good cops and crooked cops endlessly hunt good and bad guys. We can visit hell daily from the comfort of our recliner. But these offerings have an effect on our soul.

Soul-sapping fare doesn't just come in visual form. What we read and listen to matters also. When my wife, Nancy, was in undergraduate school, she got all out of sorts one semester. What was wrong? She was a whiz-bang student, majoring in English literature. She liked everything from Chaucer to the Romantics, but in order to graduate, she had to take some modern literature classes. It turned out that her Virginia Woolf class was playing havoc with her spirit.

Woolf was a depressed, tormented writer who committed suicide by walking into deep water with stones in her pockets. I'm not faulting Woolf for her mental illness. She had lived a hard life. But, by definition, she was

TALKING TO A LOVED ONE

not able to rise above it. The darkness that consumed her seeps into her works, and it's difficult, if not impossible, to read works like these without it taking a toll on your own spirit.

Misery loves company. Unfortunately, the postmodern aesthetic insists that the darker a work is, the more worthy it is of our attention. It is a phenomenon that should be exposed for what it is: a philosophy that exalts death over life, depression over joy, and insomnia over slumber.

MORE SLEEP HYGIENE COUNSEL: CUTTING OUT WHATSOEVER KILLS

I had many a postmodern teacher in my schooling, but I got lucky; I also had a few who weren't. I took entire courses in college I can't remember, but I recall an incident in an undergraduate American literature class that made my whole life better.

The teacher's name was Professor Rousseau (her real name). One day, she began class as usual, and then she veered off the trail. She opened the day's newspaper and went article by article, discussing what she felt was worth her while to read, what was a waste of her time, and what we "couldn't pay her to read" because it was detrimental. I'd never heard someone talk like this. Was she a Christian? I don't know, but the wisdom she was espousing was. I believe a good deal fewer people would have depression if they listened to her.

Jesus said that if your right hand causes you to sin, then cut it off. It would be better to enter heaven with just one hand than to go to hell with both. Likewise, he said that if your right eye causes you to sin, it would be better to pluck it out. It would be better to enter life with one eye than go to hell with two.[2] Jesus was not suggesting that we willy-nilly maim ourselves. He was telling us how much sin harms us. He was telling us how to handle the human propensity to be drawn to the things that kill us. He was telling us that life isn't a game.

I have very little willpower when I'm sitting alone in front of a television. I flip from one channel to another and then get involved with a show. When an ad comes on, I start channel surfing. Often I forget what it was I was watching in the first place. I can waste hours and not see a complete show. Afterward, I feel blank, agitated, or depressed. At night I have trouble sleeping or have strange, disturbing dreams.

When I became a Christian, I took Jesus' advice and plucked out the eye that caused me to sin by disconnecting our television. We haven't had television service for two decades. Likewise, I don't carry a computer with me when I travel, and I shut it down when I've finished work at the end of the day. Trouble sleeping can be a sign of depression; likewise, insomnia *and* depression can be signs that we're putting the wrong stuff into our brains.

The same influence visual entertainment can exert on us is equally true for the music we listen to and the stories we read. I believe that those who are depressed should be particularly careful about what they put into their minds. Of all people, they should not watch shows that glamorize suicide. And they should avoid books and other art forms by those who have committed suicide.

Instead, someone who is depressed should study the works of those who battled depression and *won*. One such person was Charles Spurgeon. Spurgeon, known as "the prince of preachers," suffered from lifelong depression. Similarly, Mother Teresa of Calcutta experienced decades of deep, chronic depression. Martin Luther, John Calvin, Handel, Charles Dickens, Florence Nightingale, Emily Dickinson, Abraham Lincoln, and many, many others have endured major depressive episodes and yet led productive lives.

If you want to become rich, would it be wise to emulate those who went bankrupt repeatedly or those who made a fortune and kept it? Similarly, I encourage my friends who are depressed to study those who have battled depression and finished the course God set before them.

A common theme among those I interviewed who had battled and beaten suicidal ideation was the habit of writing encouraging Scriptures, aphorisms, lyrics, and proverbs on paper and then taping them to walls, mirrors, refrigerators, and doors in their homes. If a friend is having trouble just getting out of bed in the morning, you might offer to write down their favorite words of encouragement and help post them around their house.

A final bit of advice on sleep: if a loved one is having trouble falling asleep, consider what a friend I deeply loved and respected told me. Ellsworth worked and taught graduate classes up until he died peacefully in his sleep at the age of ninety-two. Whenever he had trouble sleeping, he'd pray for others. He'd start down a list of family, friends, students, and neighbors, thanking God for who they were, praying for the struggles they were going through, and making intercession. He said there's no sweeter way to drift off to sleep than praying for others.

Interest (I of SIG E CAPS)
Another sign of depression is a decreased interest in the things that used to be absorbing. You might ask your loved one about what they find fun or what gets their mind off their troubles. One member of my church struggles periodically with bipolar disorder. During a recent downturn, she found herself reading the same three edifying books over and over. She said she couldn't absorb much at times, but the repetition of uplifting themes helped.

The greatest thing for all of us to have an interest in is others. Depression can drag its victims into a solitary place where it's difficult to think of anything but themselves. The goal of every Christian should be not thinking less of ourselves but thinking about ourselves less.

Of all those I talked with who have overcome suicidal thoughts, the one I believe is most successful is a friend named Rose. She was married and had supported her husband through medical school and residency. They had three children along the way. Then, at the end of residency, with no warning or indications that anything was wrong, her husband came home and said that he was leaving her to go off with a nurse he'd fallen for. Rose was devastated. She also suddenly found herself in a financial

bind. Rose went into a deep depression. She
thought about killing herself on a daily basis.
She made a plan for how she would do it.

Throughout this crisis, Rose clung to her
faith. Specifically, she clung to the assurances
of Christ, who promised never to leave her
or forsake her.[3] Ultimately, she was also held
back from committing suicide by love for her
children. What would happen to them if she
were gone?

*The interest that
people who are
depressed have in
others should be
cultivated, encouraged,
and applauded.*

Her desire to not inflict pain on others is
a common theme among those who have wrestled with suicidal thoughts
and won. Ultimately, their choice to live is predicated on a selfless concern for another's welfare. I know that some who commit suicide are in
unimaginable mental (or physical) pain, and it can be difficult in such
circumstances to think of others. But the model we have for life embodied
in Christ is one of selflessness.

Much modern psychotherapy focuses on our own happiness, needs,
wants, and desires. But what if lasting joy is found not by seeking our own
happiness but that of others? The interest that people who are depressed
have in others should be cultivated, encouraged, and applauded.
Remember the Life Continuum Scale from chapter 3? The goal of the
Christian life is not happiness. Happiness is the by-product of serving
the Lord and others. Christ could not have more clearly illustrated this
than when he undressed and washed his disciples' feet, an act of utmost
humility and selfless love.

A few years after her divorce, Rose met a pastor and fell in love.
They had a wonderful life together. Her children prospered and became
successful adults. Now in her nineties, Rose still has a spring in her step
and a gleeful glint in her eye. Each new day, she awakens to a glass half
full. She is one of the most optimistic and generous people I have ever
met. Rose attracts friends of all ages and brings neighbors to church

with her each week. She continues to find joy in her
to others.

Another suggestion for dealing with anhedon
the inability to feel pleasure from life) is to help
a memory box, scrapbook, or journal filled with memo.
has made them happy in the past. Sometimes the person needs tang
reminders of the interests that once brought them joy—and can bring
them joy again. Such mementos also remind them that their depressed
state won't go on forever.

Guilt (G of SIG E CAPS)

Those who are depressed may experience guilt and its cousin, shame. Both
shame and guilt can be powerful motivators to *avoid* sin and bad behavior. But when a loved one is ruminating on a particular event that causes
shame or guilt and is not moving forward, such thoughts can be deadly.

The Bible's take on shame and guilt is quite different from the postmodern take. Guilt in the biblical sense is our conscience and the Holy
Spirit moving us to acknowledge sin and wrongdoing and to avoid such
actions in the future. Shame is the emotion felt when we have been caught
or when we remember these wrong or sinful behaviors.

I believe that one of the reasons that Alcoholics Anonymous (AA) has
been successful in helping people with alcoholism is that the program
deals with guilt and shame head-on. First, it challenges the alcoholic to
make a "fearless" moral inventory of *what* they have done wrong and
whom they have injured. Then the program demands that these sins be
confessed to God and others. Next, the participant asks God to remove
their sins and shortcomings. Lastly, the alcoholic makes a list of those they
have harmed and makes amends.

AA's method of dealing with guilt and shame is straight out of the
pages of the Bible. One example is in the story of Zacchaeus.[4] Zacchaeus
was a tax collector and probably one of the most wicked people in the
nation of Israel. He lived in the cursed city of Jericho. The native Jews

.d him. I believe that Zacchaeus couldn't go out even in the daylight
.out his bodyguards. But Jesus came to Zacchaeus, and at the end of
.e encounter between the two, a joyful Zacchaeus confessed that he had
wronged others and promised to pay back even more than what he had
taken from them.

The person you are approaching has certainly hurt others; all of us
have. Sometimes we can apologize and make amends, and sometimes we
cannot. Sometimes people don't live long enough. Sometimes reestablish-
ing contact with someone from our past whom we have harmed would
cause more havoc than good.

I believe that everyone, especially people haunted by guilt or shame,
should take an inventory of whom they have harmed, whom they have
apologized to, and whom they have made amends to. If your list is blank,
God help you. People in the most spiritually precarious place are those
who have never apologized to God *or* others.

They are also the most spiritually immature people. Shame and guilt
don't magically go away without confession and amends. The Bible tells
us that if we confess our sins to God, "he is faithful and just to forgive us
our sins and to cleanse us from all wickedness" (1 John 1:9).

Perhaps the person you are trying to help has lashed out at you.
Repeatedly. On the surface, this doesn't seem to make sense. Why hurt
the people who love you most? At a deeper level, lashing out at others is
just one of many ways that people who are suicidal are, ultimately, hurting themselves.

Loved ones tend to forgive and forget. However, forgiveness should
not be taken for granted. It not only helps a person to acknowledge when
they have hurt others (and to apologize); it helps heal the ones they have
hurt.

Once a sin has been confessed to God and amends have been made,
the Bible advises people to move on. Remind your loved one that God
has set their sin "as far from [them] as the east is from the west" (Psalm
103:12).

Energy (E of SIG E CAPS)

Depression can also be characterized by a lack of energy. But be careful: lack of energy can also signify physical ailments. Of all the symptoms of depression that can be potentially misleading, a lack of energy comes to the top of the list.

Let me share an illustration. Nancy and I met friends for lunch several years ago. Kristen complained about a lack of energy. She had a busy life, teen children, and a thriving radio ministry. As we talked, I noticed that Kristen hardly touched her food. Her husband said that she was seeing her family doctor the next day. Her diagnosis was not depression but metastatic lung cancer (in someone who had never been exposed to smoke). Lack of energy combined with weight loss should always trigger a medical workup.

Nonetheless, a lack of energy in your loved one can be an important sign of depression. If this lack of energy is combined with a decline in activity, the depression can deepen. It is crucial for those with depression to make sure they are moving and getting exercise. There is an old saying: "Chop wood; carry water." This is sound advice for those who want to prevent or treat depression. If you want to help your friend, recommend daily, mundane physical tasks that accomplish something, like doing the dishes or vacuuming the floor. Weeding in the garden can also be therapeutic. The impact of physical movement on emotional well-being is a significant but often overlooked factor.

In the 1740s, the great Anglican evangelist John Wesley published a bestselling home health guide titled *Primitive Physick*. Much of his advice is outdated. However, I do concur with Wesley's insight that we were meant to earn our living by the sweat of our brow. Wesley believed that if we don't work up a sweat each day, we will suffer. This is sage advice for you to pass along to your loved one. Encourage them to get moving and stay moving. A depressed person doesn't have to run marathons, but taking walks and spending time outdoors are habits that heal. Help your loved one set modest and reasonable goals. To make the goals tangible, you can encourage them to keep a journal of physical chores and activities.

Concentration (C of SIG E CAPS)

People who are depressed often have difficulty concentrating on work and mental tasks. The inability to concentrate can be especially disturbing to those who take a great deal of pride in their work.

This brings me to the subject of prayer. It has been said that when we strive on our own, we do all the work. When we pray, God takes over.

If your loved one is depressed, they may have a difficult time praying. Actually, concentration and prayer can be difficult in the best of times. We live in a world that goes a million miles a second. Obviously, if your loved one has not accepted Christ as their Savior, Sanctifier, and Redeemer, they should be offered the gospel message in the terms they can understand.

Irrespective of whether they accept Christ, your desire (and God's) is that they *live*. As the Bible says, God takes no pleasure in the death of sinners. He wants them to turn from their evil.[5]

How does one pray when they can't concentrate long enough to form their thoughts? God will send the Holy Spirit to help them:

The Holy Spirit helps us in our weakness. For example, we don't know what God wants us to pray for. But the Holy Spirit prays for us with groanings that cannot be expressed in words. And the Father who knows all hearts knows what the Spirit is saying, for the Spirit pleads for us believers in harmony with God's own will.

ROMANS 8:26-27

Those who are depressed are often pointed toward the hopeful lines in Scripture, and there is nothing wrong with those lines. But the Bible also includes sections expressly reserved for the depressed. Consider the following verses from the Psalms in the poetic King James Version: "I am poured out like water, and all my bones are out of joint: my heart is like wax; it is melted in the midst of my bowels. My strength is dried up like a potsherd; and my tongue cleaveth to my jaws; and thou hast brought me into the dust of death" (Psalm 22:14-15).

My heart is like wax . . . melted in the midst of my bowels. What a powerful picture; what a prayer of misery and longing! The words from this psalm are the ones Christ called to mind while dying on the cross: "My God, my God, why have you forsaken me?" Likewise, Psalm 88 is a prayer uttered by the depressed, for the depressed. When someone who is depressed doesn't have the strength to bring their own words to mind, they can use those of the Holy Spirit. Never mind that the words aren't rosy. A connection will be opened up between the person and "the man of sorrows, who is acquainted with grief"—Christ. Indeed, that is part of the reason why these words are in Scripture!

The Bible is not an eat-only-what-pleases-you buffet. It is a balanced diet of spiritual food. Your friend needs the Bible's broccoli and carrots as well as its pizza and desserts. I can't think of a better remedy for a sudden existential melancholy than a read straight through the book of Ecclesiastes.

Appetite (A of SIG E CAPS)

Let's transition from the spiritual appetite to the physical. The person who is depressed frequently either loses their appetite or can't stop eating. As a symptom of depression, this is fairly straightforward. But it is less often included in the medical model of *causal* factors.

The first boundaries and disciplines imposed on us by our parents are going to bed when we don't want to and eating what's put on our plate. Parents who do not lovingly teach these boundaries do their children a disservice. But none of us gets to choose our parents. Perhaps you had parents who didn't teach these lessons when the stakes were no higher than sitting at the table until you finished your vegetables before you got dessert.

For these people, there is a bit of discovery to be done. The old saying "You are what you eat" is true, but so is "man does not live by bread alone."

There are many books that highlight the connection between mood and eating. If your loved one struggles with food, remember that your great-great-grandparents Adam and Eve stumbled over this block and that your great-uncle Esau had problems here as well.

Could fasting one day a week as a spiritual discipline help? Could a diet without refined sugars help stabilize moods? It is certainly something to discuss with your loved one. The Bible has a good deal to say about eating. Jesus taught for five chapters at the dinner table in the book of John, and he told us not to become obsessed by what we eat.[6] But certainly this is an area that should be explored with those who are depressed.

Psychomotor (P of SIG E CAPS)

The P of SIG E CAPS stands for psychomotor changes. Those who are depressed can appear to slow down in their movements, and this can have the effect of making them appear older than they are. Likewise, they can become fidgety and agitated. They may pace or repeat tic-like movements such as chewing their nails, twirling their hair, or bobbing their foot.

What therapeutic insights can we get from these psychomotor changes? Just a generation ago, the saying "idle hands are the devil's workshop" was thought to be sage advice. How can you help your loved one's hands (and nervous energy) be put to God's use? Earlier we talked about taking an interest in others. Knit one, purl two will not only result in a scarf that can be given away; the act itself can help ease their depression. What are other ways your loved one could put their hands to use in service of someone else?

Suicidal Ideation (S of SIG E CAPS)

Lastly, suicidal thoughts are a concerning and consistent pattern of those suffering a major depressive episode. As we've discussed previously, these thoughts originated in the Garden when we failed to heed God's warning. Taking that first bite was a suicidal act. It resulted in immediate spiritual death (separation from God) and in physical death (mortality). Always take any expression of suicidal intent seriously, as we saw earlier in this chapter (see pages 123–124). Seek help right away.

WHERE THE RUBBER HITS THE TARMAC

I recently was flying home on a small commuter jet with two seats on either side of the aisle. I was by the window. A mother sat next to me, and her two sons sat across the aisle. She wanted to talk, so I listened. Her life was wrapped up in the athletic success of her sons, ages ten and thirteen. They flew constantly to events, training camps, and practice sessions.

When we were nearly home, she asked me what I did for a living. I told her I was a Christian writer. She asked what I was writing, and I told her that I was working on a book about suicide.

She lowered her voice and told me that her thirteen-year-old had told her just the week before that he didn't want to live anymore.

"How did you respond?" I questioned.

"I told him not to say that. Look at all the opportunities you have that other children don't. Look at all your parents are doing for you," she continued.

My hand on a Bible, this is a verbatim retelling of the story. How would you respond to her? What would you say to her son? How would you bring up faith? Being prepared for situations like this is the whole point of this chapter and, I believe, the obligation of every Christian.

We started this chapter by stating this is the part of the book where the rubber meets the road, and now we end it with the tire touching down on the tarmac. Obviously, this mother did not intend harm to her children. But I believe this story shows us the necessity of being prepared beforehand to

Every Christian needs to be prepared to help save a friend who is over their head in the sea of depression.

have these conversations when they arise. Her response is an example of what *not* to do when a loved one says they want to die. We can learn just as much from bad examples as good ones. How we approach someone who might be suicidal can be a matter of life or death.

This chapter has been a starting point for anyone concerned about a loved one who is depressed. If you don't have anyone in your life that is suicidal now, you are fortunate. However, I don't know anyone in the second half of life whom suicide has not touched.

In *The Weight of Glory*, C. S. Lewis argues that all Christians have a duty to save a drowning man. Lewis further argues that if we live on the coast, we may have a duty to learn lifesaving so that we are prepared to save any drowning man who shows up.

When it comes to suicide, we are all living on the coast. Every Christian needs to be prepared to help save a friend who is over their head in the sea of depression.

This chapter has given you some tools to determine if a friend is in immediate danger and to begin offering resources and help. In the next chapter, we will take a closer look at how the church can reach out to people who are in pain and collectively be better prepared to save lives.

CHAPTER 9

Pastors and Suicide

WHAT THEY DIDN'T TEACH YOU IN SEMINARY

※

I suppose some brethren neither have much
elevation or depression. I could almost wish to share
their peaceful life, for I am much tossed up and down,
and although my joy is greater than the most of men, my
depression of spirit is such as few can have an idea of.

CHARLES SPURGEON

WHENEVER I AM EXPERIENCING an inconvenience in ministry and I start to be ungrateful, I think about the apostle Paul's travails. Five times he received thirty-nine lashes, and three times he was beaten with rods. At Lystra, Paul was stoned by the townspeople, dragged outside the city gates, and left for dead. Three times Paul was shipwrecked. Once he spent a day and a night drifting in the sea, clinging to debris. He went hungry and thirsty, was chained to prison walls, spent sleepless nights in agony, was abandoned, betrayed, and longed for his warm cloak as his breath condensed in the dank air of dungeons.[1] As he suffered all these torments, he gazed on a world that was a complete blur with one face looking like every other, because another of Paul's misfortunes was that he could barely see. Paul lived more than a thousand years before eyeglasses were invented.

Paul wasn't looking for pity or sympathy when he recounted his ordeals to the church. He was establishing his bona fides, his credentials to give the church advice. In this chapter, I will talk about what the church can do to battle the awful plague of suicide that has killed so many in our churches, our nation, and our world.

What are my credentials for offering guidance to the church? First, let me tell you what I am not. I am not a megachurch pastor. I am not the head of a denomination. I have never graduated from a Sunday school class, much less a seminary. My only theological credential is an honorary doctorate from Hood Theological Seminary, an African Methodist Episcopal Zion institution—a degree I treasure as highly as my medical degree. Yet I have had the privilege to preach on multiple occasions at the Washington National Cathedral, at governors' and mayors' prayer breakfasts, at megachurches and micro churches, at home churches, at schools and universities, to the military, and to Catholics and Protestants. On multiple occasions, I have been privileged to teach entire seminary faculties. I have given talks where I was the only one who spoke English, the only one over thirty, the only one under seventy, the only male, and the only Christian. Whether I am speaking to grade school children or retirees, I am equally honored to represent Jesus Christ.

> *Pastors and churches must become engaged in the battle for the lives and the souls of those who are contemplating suicide. This must start from the top and work its way down, and it also must rise up from the bottom.*

Even when I am teaching within the walls of a church building or a chapel, I frequently find myself speaking as an outsider. Whether I am addressing a group that claims to hold the Bible as God's inerrant Word or one that has decided that it can correct God, I have spoken the truth as I have found it revealed throughout the entire Bible. This is often equally challenging to both groups.

Through these experiences, I have been given the unusual gift of friendships across the entire bandwidth of the church. Like Paul, I say these things not to boast, but to establish that my love and concern for God's church consumes me. I believe that one day I will stand before God and answer for every word I have spoken, and for every word in this book.

And so, it is with trepidation and wonder that I offer guidance on the subject of suicide. Pastors and churches must become engaged in the battle for the lives and the souls of those who are contemplating suicide. This must start from the top and work its way down, and it also must rise up from the bottom. In this chapter I will address pastors and priests. In the following chapter I will address lay leaders and the church.

SERMONS AND FUNERALS

To date, I have not met anyone who attends church who has heard a sermon about why suicide is wrong. I have also asked friends who are pastors, and not one of them has delivered a sermon on this topic. This does not mean that no pastors are preaching about suicide, but it does mean that not many are.

Some congregants have heard sermons *after* someone has committed suicide, and it is important to offer comfort to those left behind, but by definition, a sermon at that point is too late. Pastors need to speak out about suicide proactively.

Having preached at the funeral of someone who committed suicide who did not believe in God, and whose family and friends were also atheists, I can think of no harder task for a pastor or priest. It is a sham to "preach someone into heaven" after their death who had no regard for the Kingdom of God in life.

Someone who has trusted in the Lord in life has reason to hope for God's mercy in death—even if they themselves were the instruments of that death.[2] But for those who held God in little or no regard, I do not believe it is biblical to promise those left behind that their loved one is "in a better place now." While the motivation might be benevolent, the outcome could be deadly. Removing a potential deterrent for anyone in the pews who is likewise contemplating suicide could have lethal consequences. I know of a number of people who were on the verge of suicide—one with a loaded gun pointed at his head—who report being given a vision of hell that stopped them.

When we think of those who have committed suicide, it is always appropriate to plead their case before God.[3] In fact, this can be a major focus of a funeral for a nonbeliever. But it is also dishonest to represent eternity as a place where we will not be judged.

No one in the Bible talks more about judgment, or about heaven and hell, than the one who has the job of doing the judging: Jesus Christ. Jesus warns us that the time to cast our lot in with him will come to an end, that the reaction by those judged "guilty" will be sorrowful, and that those cast into hell cannot get out.[4] For many today, the only time they might hear the truth about the gospel and eternity is at a funeral.

A dozen years ago, a group of Roman Catholic priests put Nancy and me up while we were traveling through Texas. I cannot remember the order they belonged to, but they rotated between Texas and San Pedro Sula, Honduras. Two of the priests described the difficulty of their work in that city torn by murder and gang violence. Often they would perform a dozen funerals a week for murdered gang members. There seemed to be little time for anything else. They realized that they would have to preach the gospel during the funerals or the gangs would never hear it.

Likewise, I believe that all pastors should write and have funeral sermons prepared in advance for both believers and nonbelievers who have committed suicide. The funeral may be the only opportunity for many to hear the gospel. While it should offer comfort where possible, it should also make clear that every one of us must place our hope in Christ and Christ alone. He is the only person in all of history who claims to be God's only begotten Son and to have defeated death. As if that were not enough, he also claims to be responsible for judging all the earth. These sermons should be prepared well in advance in a time of calm contemplation and prayer, guided by the Holy Spirit.

It is always easier to lay down rules and set boundaries *before* they are needed. As an example, while preaching in a megachurch in Florida,

I recall the senior pastor instructing the entire congregation, "I will not preach at your funeral if you want the song 'I Did It My Way' played. The song is against everything Christianity stands for. Christians do it God's way—period—so don't even ask me." It was far easier for the pastor to set this boundary preemptively rather than in the midst of consoling a family immediately after they lost a loved one.

ARTICULATING A BIBLICALLY SOUND THEOLOGY OF SUICIDE

The pastor should be clear that suicide is wrong. Suicide is Satan's plan for our lives, not Christ's. Death by suicide results when people listen to Satan's lies, not God's truth.

There is a lot of bad theology floating around the internet concerning suicide. Some of it even gets printed, and, sadly, some of it is taught in seminaries. One way to discern if the writers have actually studied Scripture is to see if they skip the account of Adam and Eve, or if they list the deaths of Saul and Samson as suicides. Another is to see if the authors criticize the church's attempts to stop suicide clusters in the era before modern medicine.

Let's consider one of the most gruesome examples. In the Middle Ages, the church was tasked with preventing suicide. They would sometimes hang the naked body of someone who had committed suicide from the city gate as a deterrent to others. This method may seem grisly and unseemly today, but it was sometimes the only thing that could stop a rash of suicides in an era before pharmacological treatments for depression were invented. Similarly, a priest heating the keys of the cathedral in a fire and pressing them into a child's arm seems like a picture of torture when taken out of context today, but during the Middle Ages right up until the time of Louis Pasteur, this treatment for a rabid dog bite decreased the rabies infection rate by an order of magnitude. What looks to us today like torture was the only effective treatment available, and it saved lives.

As I've argued throughout this book, suicide is a sin that causes real harm to others. While these methods are not what I would prescribe today, the problem is no less serious, so we need to be clear in articulating a biblical worldview about suicide.

When pastors begin in ministry, they often have thin skin. They worry about receiving criticism or upsetting the apple cart. Over time, however, a good pastor should aim to grow a tougher skin and a more tender heart. We must be clear about the sin of suicide while also loving and caring for those who are considering it in our midst.

Nearly every pastor is called upon to counsel the depressed and suicidal, yet some have less training in that area than they do in Hebrew.

Pastors need to remember that theologians tell us what they've read and that saints tell us what they've seen. The goal of a pastor is to help form saints. Every pastor should have an example of someone who struggled with depression and suicide and prevailed in their faith. If you are too early in your career to have met someone personally, then use Spurgeon or one of the other heroes of the faith (see pages 187–191). Anyone who has prevailed against suicide and come out on the other side with their faith stronger is, in my book, a hero and a saint. They have seen the power of God at work.

TRAINING

I've never heard of a pastor being approached by a parishioner struggling with the translation of a line from the Bible in Greek or Hebrew. Yet many pastors have spent whole semesters studying those subjects. I would not discourage any from their study. But nearly every pastor is called upon to counsel the depressed and suicidal, yet some have less training in that area than they do in Hebrew.

Every pastor should have some schooling or coaching on how to counsel depressed and suicidal people. Pastors called to this area should invest in formal training as well. They should learn the various systems

defense mechanisms are, and when people use them.
ble to spot those with personality disorders and train
how to approach situations that frequently arise with
epressed or suicidal. (The information in chapter 4 may
rting point.)

is not trained or equipped to help those with mental illness,
have a ready referral at hand and a book or two to recom-
eve that no pastor should attempt counseling someone of the
x unless they have a vast amount of training and can recognize
e and countertransference, *and* they have a therapy supervisor,
hiatrists do. Too many ministries have been wrecked by welled clergy who crossed a line they didn't anticipate in advance.

nal Hazards

imes surprised by dedicated Christians who have never taken the
ead through the Bible, paying close attention to what it says about
their particular occupation. Whether it be teachers, soldiers, merchants,
or mothers, the Bible has wisdom to offer. By failing to investigate what
God teaches about their callings, they have not only shortchanged their
faith; they have shortchanged their profession.

No occupation is more represented in Scripture than that of ministry. Where did Moses go wrong? When
did Jonah, or Peter, or Paul make a mistake?
What did they do right? How did they man-
age a bad situation?

Pastors who actually live out what Christ
experienced will find that the Gospels come
alive. For example, perhaps a pastor preached
his heart out and had someone subsequently
give their life to Christ—and then received a
complaint about the sermon. Similarly, Jesus
frequently was bashed for boldly speaking

*Clergy are not immune
to depression or suicidal
thoughts. If and when
such thoughts come,
clergy should be
encouraged to get help.*

God's truth,[5] so we should not be surprised when this happens to pastors today, too.

If clergy consistently preach the gospel in love, people will come. More important, God will show up. Nonetheless, it is inevitable that pastors will encounter dark days at work. The parable of the wheat and the tares is all too real. Clergy are not immune to depression or suicidal thoughts. If and when such thoughts come, clergy should be encouraged to seek counsel and get help.

As a preventative measure, it can be helpful to read the works or biographies of pastors who struggled with depression but did not let it master them. The writings of Frederick Buechner (especially his three autobiographical works where he talks about the impact of his father committing suicide), Martin Luther, Charles Spurgeon, Mother Teresa, and Henri Nouwen will let clergy know that they are not alone in their struggles. It is also important to have relationships in place with counselors and spiritual advisers *before* a crisis hits. Developing a trusting relationship and getting periodic checkups is always good medicine for the body as well as the spirit.

The church has seen several high-profile pastor suicides in recent years, and each is a tragedy. Beyond this number, there are many, many pastors who are beaten down and beleaguered by their task. Ministry is a hard job, beset by temptation, difficulty, and weariness. What follows is advice for pastors designed to help prevent the desperation that can lead to suicide.

Addictions

If a pastor is having trouble with alcohol or drugs, they should join a 12-step program. As clergy, they will know that their "higher power" isn't a doorknob but a man of sorrows who is acquainted with their grief. It may not be a coincidence that the sources of warmth and heat in churches are often located in the basements—this includes not only the furnace, but the AA and Celebrate Recovery groups that meet there.

If pastors are having trouble with pornography, they should consider getting rid of their computers. Ministerial life went along just fine for a couple of thousand years without them. At the very least, they should put safeguards in place to make their computer usage an open book.

I know two men who carry only a "dumb" flip phone and eschew computers. Although neither is a cleric, both are extremely devoted Christians who use their hundreds of millions of dollars to build up the church. People can be successful—materially and spiritually—without the latest technology.

Fellowship

Pastors should surround themselves with others who seek the Kingdom of Heaven above all else. Birds of a feather flock together. Clergy should fly in the center of this flock.

I would not survive in ministry were it not for the sacred friendships God has allowed me to have. It is all too common for pastors to report feeling isolated and lonely. A providential friendship is a thing worthy of getting on your knees and asking the Lord for. The Bible and close friends should be like sandpaper: constantly challenging and always helping to make rough places planed. When that stops being the case, the pastor has stopped growing. In this sense, being a Christian is like being a shark; when we stop moving forward, we die.

Integrity

Every pastor should have thought through and discussed with a peer or supervisor the lines they won't cross and the compromises they won't make. When these lines are supported by Scripture, the pastor is standing on a rock.

I recall meeting a man many years ago who had just graduated from seminary with his master's in divinity. It had been his long-term dream to become a pastor of a local church, and he had spent years on the journey. A week before graduation, his wife of six years said that she was leaving him to pursue her own dreams.

The first thing he did was to call the church that had offered him a job and turn it down. He referenced 1 Timothy 3:2: "A bishop [pastor] then must be blameless, the husband of one wife, vigilant, sober, of good behaviour, given to hospitality, apt to teach" (KJV). This man interpreted 1 Timothy to mean that a divorced person should not be the pastor of a church.

This line has been changed in many modern translations and interpretations. Some feel that it only applies to those who had multiple wives at the same time, i.e., those in polygamous marriages. Nonetheless, this gentleman felt that it precluded him from serving in the pastor's role, and I respect him for his integrity. It cost him much, but he knew there were other ways he could use his education to serve the Kingdom.

Imagine if everyone held themselves to the authority of God as they understood it to be revealed in Scripture. Let me explain how his integrity helped someone else in ministry.

True story: One June, I received an invitation to go to Baltimore, Maryland, and speak to high school principals the following July (i.e., in thirteen months). The dates were clear on my calendar, and my staff accepted the invitation. A day later, I received an invitation from the Prince of Wales to meet with him and some other church leaders and stay at his castle at the exact time I was to speak to the principals.

What would you do? I debated for a day: downtown Baltimore in July versus a castle in the British countryside is hardly an even contest. The principals' event was still over a year away, and they had plenty of time to find a replacement. It would be so easy to make an excuse and retract my acceptance. Yet when I remembered the man who took himself out of the running for the pastorate, I knew what I had to do. I turned down the prince and kept my commitment to Baltimore. I have met thousands of pastors, but the lesson this recent seminary graduate taught me about personal integrity has never left me. Imagine how much better the world would be if everyone's yes was yes and no was no.

Another piece of advice for pastors on the issue of integrity: pastors should strive to live below their means. A humbler-than-necessary lifestyle keeps options open and makes it possible for clergy to maintain their witness.

Taking a Break When Needed

Ministry is hard, and I fear it will only become more so in the future. When pastors find themselves overwhelmed, depressed, or suicidal, they should step aside. God does not love anyone because of the work they do. He loves us because he loves us.

In the long run, it is far more important for the pastor to take a break and get healthy. Both the pastor and the church will benefit. The suicide of a clergy member is not only a tragedy; it is a sermon—the worst kind that can be made. The Bible says that we who teach the Bible will be judged more harshly than those who believe but do not take a leader's role.[6]

In chapter 6, I talked about the HALT systems check that we taught our children to determine if they were out of sorts because they were hungry, angry, lonely, or tired. The HALT method can be valuable for pastors, too, in determining if and when it is time to take a break. Elijah was pushed to the point of desperation because he was all four—hungry, angry, lonely, and tired. It is better to take a break than to do something that will harm a pastor's reputation, witness, ministry, or congregation.

Pastors, perhaps more than anyone, need to remember that God's rest is more powerful than our work.

The Importance of Sabbath

Lastly, of the many, many pastors I have met, those who regularly keep a Sabbath (as opposed to just a day off) are healthier and more mentally fit. While a day off is great, a Sabbath is something even more wonderful: it's a gift from the Lord we are invited to open fifty-two times a year, a day focused on holy rest.[7] Ministry is a marathon, not a sprint. I know scientifically, anecdotally, and from personal experience that Sabbath keeping can be one of the cornerstones of a healthy ministry. A church needs a pastor who needs God more than they need anything else—including work. Setting one day a week aside for God and holy rest is not optional; it's one of God's top ten commandments. Blatantly rebelling against any of the other nine commandments would get a pastor fired. Pastors, perhaps more than anyone, need to remember that God's rest is more powerful than our work. It bears repeating: When we work, we work. When we pray, God works.

KEEPING YOUR EYES ON THE PRIZE

A decade ago, a church asked me to go on retreat with thirty leaders and the pastoral staff. We spent three days in a beautiful mountain setting. They were wrestling with a problem that many churches would be glad to have: what to do with the tens of millions of dollars they were to receive from the sale of an urban property. They didn't think God wanted them to spend the money on themselves. They wanted to be good stewards. They wanted to spend the money on things that would have a lasting impact and took their charge seriously.

I was honored to spend the weekend with them. For the most part, my task was invigorating, with one exception. A longtime member of the church was an ardent naysayer. He loved to argue and play the part of the spoiler. Even when someone tried to agree with him, he found a way to disagree. His negativity was unrelenting.

After three days, a heretical thought crossed my mind. Would the church be better off if this man's pastor invited him to the church basement, found an excuse to head back up the stairs, and then locked the door behind him?

I had this thought after only three days with the naysayer. Yet there was his pastor, patience personified, lovingly intervening and redirecting—and he'd been dealing with this parishioner for twenty years!

The moral of the story was crystal clear. Being a local church pastor takes more patience and perseverance than I could ever summon. My job as an itinerant pastor is easy. If you are a local church pastor, your job is hard. Very hard.

I'll close with a caution not from me, but from God to Ezekiel. It applies directly to every pastor responsible for shepherding a flock today:

> I have made [you] a watchman for the house of Israel. Whenever you hear a word from my mouth, you shall give them warning from me. If I say to the wicked, O wicked one, you shall surely die, and you do not speak to warn the wicked to turn from his way, that wicked person shall die in his iniquity, but his blood I will require at your hand. But if you warn the wicked to turn from his way, and he does not turn from his way, that person shall die in his iniquity, but you will have delivered your soul.
> EZEKIEL 33:7-9, ESV

Beloved pastor, never lose track of what your job is about. If I did my job right in the emergency department, someone might gain a few decades of life. If you get it right, someone gains eternity. In the case of suicide, the medical world needs you to help keep people alive so that they can hear the words of eternal life.

CHAPTER 10

The Church and Suicide

WHAT WE DIDN'T LEARN IN SUNDAY SCHOOL

※

He comforts us in all our troubles so that we can
comfort others. When they are troubled, we will be able
to give them the same comfort God has given us.

2 CORINTHIANS 1:4

I LOVE STORIES of the church in action. A few years ago, a pastor told me a story that's illustrative for lay leaders who want to be part of the solution to our suicide crisis but don't know where or how to start.

A couple in this pastor's church felt called to become foster parents. To qualify, they participated in home visits and a series of training sessions. Toward the end of the training, they were required to accompany a social worker and the sheriff as they forcibly removed a child from an unsafe home.

In each of these extractions, the children were given a large garbage bag and told they had ten minutes to collect their valuables and keepsakes. The couple from the church was brokenhearted after witnessing several of these "extractions." It was tragic enough that children were taken from homes and whisked away to places they had never been. That couldn't be helped. And it was sad that all they took with them was what they could gather in a ten-minute period. But what really irked them was that the children had to transport all their possessions in a garbage bag.

The unintended message to the children was that all they owned, and perhaps all they were, was trash. The couple got to work, and with the help of the pastor, others in the church, and the county child protective services, they changed things. Now, if any child in the county is taken from a home, they are first given a new suitcase emblazoned with their name.

Churches can move mountains, and they can save lives. Jesus taught about this in the parable of the Good Samaritan. Like the Good Samaritan, the first step for us in the church is to get off our donkeys and do something.

The object of this book is to get the church moving, not to supply all the answers. Any book or program that claims to have all the answers to mental illness is suspect and should be avoided.

Like the Good Samaritan, the first step for us in the church is to get off our donkeys and do something.

As a starting point, it is helpful for a church to identify and consult in-house experts. Most churches have a family physician, general internist, emergency doctor, psychiatrist, psychiatric social worker, psychiatric nurse, or school counselor among them. These people should be consulted when discussing how the church can help people who are depressed or suicidal. Below are some areas for the church to consider, pray about, and act upon.

SMALL GROUP STUDY

Before enacting any change in the church, it is helpful to gather a group of people interested in the topic to study what the Bible says. This can take the form of a Sunday school class, book group, or small group study. A Bible study on depression and mental illness will help plow the ground for future action. The group can be led by the pastor, a church member with training in counseling or medicine, or an outside expert. You can use a book such as this, any of the books listed in the resource section (see pages 197–199), or a book recommended by your in-house experts.

Those who have successfully battled depression or helped a loved one with depression can be invited to share their story and what worked for them. We should help carry each other's burdens. Satan loves lies and deception. He can be defeated only when we open the door and let God's truth shine on the burdens we carry.

SUPPORT GROUPS

Dealing and living with those who suffer from mental illness is taxing. Could your church host a support and prayer group for the loved ones of those with mental illness?

It is also helpful to host support groups for those suffering from mental illness or addictions. Do you host AA, Al-Anon, or Celebrate Recovery groups? Has your church reached out to veterans who are struggling? Recently divorced people? Those who have lost a spouse? All these populations are at greater than average risk for depression and suicide.

We once belonged to a church where someone began to sign the pastor's sermons for those who were hard of hearing. The remarkable thing was that no one in the church was hard of hearing at the time. Within several months, however, that changed, and a half dozen sat facing the one signing.

If your church develops support groups for those with mental illness or their caregivers, it is 100 percent certain that someone in the church already needs it, and you may draw others in as well. You may not be able to cure the illness, but you can be a part of a healing process.

A MINISTRY OF PRESENCE

People with mental illness have much to contribute to the church. If I were going to name a ministry in a church tasked with connecting with these folks, I might call it the Spurgeon Ministry. As I mentioned earlier, Charles Spurgeon, the prince of preachers, struggled with major depression, and yet he is almost without peer in preaching circles.[1]

Sometimes a ministry of presence is what is most needed. One emergency department I worked in for a dozen years had a regular visitor with schizophrenia. Our department provided the regular injections of anti-psychotic medications that were prescribed for her. Often she would sit in the waiting room at night, just wanting to be near others.

Shortly after I started working in the department, I went out to the waiting room in the wee hours of the morning, sat down, and got to know her. She knit to keep her hands busy. When I told her I had learned how to knit as a kid, she opened her bag and handed me needles and yarn.

Over the years, we spent countless hours knitting in the middle of the night. She was the first Christian I knew with serious mental illness. I was not a believer at the time, but I was astounded by how much better she was because of her faith—even in her rough seasons. I won't be a bit surprised to meet her in heaven and to find out that God sent her to help me.

One of the reasons that Christians have been much less likely to commit suicide is because they have a sense of belonging. Our society is fractured. Finding ways to connect with hurting teens through Big Brothers Big Sisters programs, reaching out to lonely widows and widowers, and welcoming people who have recently been divorced are just a few of the many ways we can identify and welcome the depressed among us. Such initiatives will benefit both the givers and receivers of loving friendship.

TRAINING

With a little research, you can identify groups in your region that specialize in training laypeople in peer-to-peer prayer and counseling. You may even have that expertise within your church. If reaching the depressed and suicidal among you is a priority, a weekend training, or series of weekly trainings, can greatly expand your capacity to help.

CHURCH POLICY

Every youth pastor, small group leader, church elder, college minister, board member, and Sunday school teacher should know what to do if they encounter a person who may be suicidal. They should be told exactly what questions to ask and what steps to take. This policy should be in writing and shared widely. A sample policy can be found in the tool kit section (page 200) and adapted for your church. This policy is meant to serve only as an example; each church should develop a policy that meets the requirements of their particular population and review it with trusted mental health and legal professionals before publishing.

PRAYER MINISTRIES

Prayer is an important way to help people suffering from depression. Our church, like many others, offers a prayer room with trained lay leaders who are available to pray with someone before, during, or after a worship service. Confessing or sharing our troubles with someone is often an important part of the healing process. These volunteers should be trained on what to do if they suspect someone is suicidal.

Some cautions:

The human mind is complicated because it is connected to a human soul. We battle against all the seen complications of life and against the unseen. "For we are not fighting against flesh-and-blood enemies, but against evil rulers and authorities of the unseen world, against mighty powers in this dark world, and against evil spirits in the heavenly places" (Ephesians 6:12).

When someone experiences depression, a spiritual cause should be considered. Sin has a way of eating away at us. But assigning spiritual blame is a pathway that should be walked with great caution. At the end of that trail, spiritual cults can be found.

In the course of interviewing people for this book, I met two who had been urged to stop their psychiatric medicines by well-intentioned people dabbling in faith healing. It was a disaster. Never encourage anyone to stop psychiatric medicines without the knowledge of the prescriber.

Nonetheless, when we are depressed we should at least consider that problems we are experiencing may be God rapping our knuckles to get our attention. Are we headed in the wrong direction? As we discussed in chapter 5 in the story of Job, sometimes we need to acknowledge that we are—at least to some degree—the authors of our own problems. While depression can be due to internal or external circumstances beyond our control, we should at least ask ourselves what we could be doing to eliminate sin from our lives.

HEALING PRAYER

For many years, a healing prayer ministry used our offices in the evenings. The ministry was the joint project of eight churches. They used our downtown office because it was located in a secular building—not a church, which they felt might intimidate some.

Those working in the ministry went through rigorous mandatory screening and training. They did no counseling. They charged no money. They did not discuss problems in depth with those seeking prayer. Women would meet with two women and men with two men when they prayed.

Any new individual coming to the prayer ministry was asked to fill out a form, giving their name, age, address, and the reason they were seeking prayer. The form clarified that they were not being offered professional counseling, that this was not therapy, and that they were there to receive prayer. The form was given to those who would be praying for them, and the two would pray for spiritual guidance before they met the person seeking prayer. The reasons people came were anything from anxiety, to suicidal thoughts, to family problems, to terminal cancer. The ministry simply prayed for those seeking help—and it worked.

One success story involved two men in their late twenties. They had planned to talk with someone before they went to a liquor store, got something to drink, and drove their car into a lake to kill themselves. Neither man was a Christian. The men were sent to two different rooms. Both prayer groups discerned that the men were suicidal, both men were offered the gospel, and both accepted the Lord on the spot. Both are alive today.

If your church develops a prayer ministry, people will come. Offer training, proceed with due caution, and have plenty of Bibles and tissues on hand.

HOSPITALITY

How does a church welcome newcomers and make members feel at home? I recall preaching at a megachurch in Michigan. About eleven thousand people attended the multiple services that day. The person leading the worship music had flown in from England. He was fantastic. At the end of the last service, the church emptied, and he and I were left standing alone. No one invited us to eat. We decided to have lunch together and pick up anyone we saw hanging about. Five of us eventually made our way to a restaurant.

I still remember the feeling of loneliness when everyone cleared out—and I was the preacher that day! What must someone who is just visiting feel like? If the visitor is already depressed or contemplating suicide, multiply my discomfort a thousandfold and then consider ways you might tweak your ministry to visitors.

In the parable of the sheep and the goats, when Jesus separates the people of the nations into the damned and the saved, the first thing he mentions is being offered a meal and a drink by those who didn't recognize him. He also says, "I was a stranger and you welcomed me." In addition to this, remember that the damned forgot to offer food and drink, and he says to them, "Depart from me!"[2]

A median-sized church in America has seventy-five people in attendance on a Sunday. Each Sunday, someone should have the task of inviting any visitor home to eat or inviting them out for lunch. They should also be on the lookout for church members who need company. Make sure you pick up the tab when you are with them. And absolutely, positively be certain to pick up the bill when you are with non-Christians.

Some of the healthiest churches where I have preached eat together weekly. The meal can take place before, between, or after services. Eating does not have to involve anything dramatic. Sandwiches can do, but remember, you might be welcoming the Lord. And don't forget to invite the pastor!

I have also preached at churches that offer a meal and worship one evening a week for the homeless. The homeless population has a higher than average concentration of people suffering from depression and suicidal ideation. Treating these people with dignity over a shared meal is a very practical way your church can nourish bodies and spirits while possibly saving a life.

Churches and their members are called by the Lord to show hospitality because it reflects the gracious love of our Lord. We should always be fighting to preserve life and bring shalom to our neighborhoods, towns, and world.

With this in mind, I would urge the church to practice, preach, and advocate for two areas that at first glance might seem to have little to do with our nation's ballooning suicide rate, but I believe they are directly connected.

SABBATH

The first topic is Sabbath. People are healthier and happier if they keep a Sabbath day, setting aside one day each week to rest and glory in the Lord. People who keep a regular Sabbath, such as Seventh-day Adventists, have been shown to live longer. Sabbath keeping also is associated with a higher quality of life as well as increased spiritual well-being.[3]

Having said this, as I read the Bible, Sabbath keeping does not affect our salvation *per se*. Sabbath keeping is not a condition of getting into heaven; it just happens to be the condition of heaven when we get there.

Sabbath keeping is not a condition of getting into heaven; it just happens to be the condition of heaven when we get there.

While it is true that Christians are no longer under judgment of the law, the law, especially the Ten Commandments, is a gift from God to humanity to help keep civilization civil.

Sabbath is a piece of real estate in time deeded to the church. No society has ever come up with the equivalent of the biblical Sabbath without having met a Christian or a Jew. The reason the church has always maintained support of Sabbath is because the Sabbath provides protection for the weakest and most voiceless in society. Even animals find protection under its umbrella.

Resting one day out of seven can only be advocated for by the church. No government or scientific agency will defend it. It is a piece of heaven right here on earth.

On the seventh day, the Lord finished his work, and he rested from all his work. He declared the day holy. God rests; God is holy; therefore, rest is holy. It is the longest commandment in the Bible, and the only one that God specially applies to himself.

> *A church cannot be for life but against the things that God designed to support life.*

Jesus is the Lord of the Sabbath, and he should be our Lord. A church should emulate God. God wove Sabbath into the fabric of the universe. We should learn to rest under this fabric in time. "For thus said the Lord GOD, the Holy One of Israel, 'In returning and rest you shall be saved; in quietness and in trust shall be your strength'" (Isaiah 30:15, ESV).

CREATION CARE

The second topic the church needs to practice, preach, and advocate for is creation care. Environmental matters have a bearing on suicide, and in particular, they disproportionately impact the next generation.

Sadly, at least part of the church has turned its back on God's creation. A church cannot be for life but against the things that God designed to support life. Young people are especially apt at recognizing hypocrisy. How can the church tell someone to reject suicide in favor of life and then at the same time maintain that they don't care what happens to life on God's creation?

Anyone who says that the Bible does not tell us to respect the environment is reading a different Bible than I have. The Lord says that he will return and destroy those who have destroyed the earth.[4]

When the Lord does return to judge the earth, the Bible tells us that people hide in caves in fear of God, but the trees of the forest shout for joy. A just judge is finally on the bench, and the trees know the ruling will be in their favor.[5]

Jesus tells his listeners that not even a single sparrow falls from the sky without our heavenly Father groaning.[6] If you have ever hit a bird while driving in a car and groaned, rest assured that the feeling in the pit of your stomach comes from God.

Jesus goes on to tell us how much more we mean to God. But to stop there is to miss the point. What Jesus is saying is this: How can you get your head around how much God loves you if you can't understand how much he loves a sparrow? God even makes room for sparrows in his holy temple![7]

I bring up this subject because many young people I speak with are leaving the church in despair. They believe that the church does not care what happens to them or the planet they will inhabit in the future. Sadly, that is true, but only for part of the church, and not for God whatsoever.

One way I connect with young people is to talk about God's love for trees. Trees are mentioned more in Scripture than any other living thing other than God and people. There is a tree on the first page of the Bible; the first psalm tells us to be like a tree; the first page of the New Testament has a tree within Jesus' family tree; and the last page of the Bible has a tree that bears fruit in every season, with leaves that will heal the nations. Reaching that tree is to be the goal of every Christian.

The only thing Jesus ever harms is a tree, and the only thing that can harm Jesus is a tree. The Bible calls itself and its wisdom a tree.[8] The only aesthetic God the Father assigns specifically in the Bible is a tree. (A tree is "pleasant to the sight" of the Lord—Genesis 2:9, ESV.) I could go on and on—in fact, I've written a book about the trees in the Bible[9]—but the point is that we need to be able to appreciate the beauty of life, including the splendor of God's creation. If we love the Creator, we should respect his creation.

I believe that God is all powerful. He can do anything he can think of. I believe that God sent his only Son so that we would have access to the tree of life.[10] God wants us to accept his free gift of eternal life and salvation and to spend eternity with him in heaven. But we must ask ourselves: *If God can do anything he wants, and if he wants us in heaven with him for eternity, why weren't we just born in heaven?*

Puzzling through this question will quickly lead one to the conclusion that this life, and this earth on which every generation must live, is a gift. It is not disposable. I believe that one day I will be given a new body in heaven. But that does not mean I should stop brushing and flossing my teeth every night. If we are faithful in little things, we will be given more. The church must be for what God is for, and he is for life.

This is not to say that the church should concentrate only on preventing suicide, or advocating for creation care, or getting people to say the sinner's prayer. God is more beautiful, more complicated, and more lovely than all the books on the planet can detail.

HOPE ALWAYS

The early church was made of people like you and me. When Jesus was captured by the police, his followers scattered. When Peter was asked if he was one of Jesus' followers, he swore, "I never knew the man!"

Yet only a short while later, Peter was willing to stand up to the police even if they beat him to death. Why? Because he had seen a man come back from the dead with his own eyes. This is what gave him and others the courage and hope to spread the gospel.

We need to see men and women come back from the dead too. This is what will happen when you and your church get involved in the lives of those who are suicidal. Spread the news. Tell all the world. Jesus died so that we can have life, and life more abundantly. Jesus died on the cross so we can have hope.

I thank God that you have cared enough about your neighbor to tackle this weighty subject with me. Bear with me a moment longer, as I close the same way that I opened this book, with a dedication to you, my patient readers, and to God's bride, the church:

❀

To you who struggle and struggled and endure

Bearing a cross upon your shoulders,

The weight known only to God;

We who love and have loved you,

Salute you,

And cry tears of thanks that God

Has given you the strength and courage to see

Another day.

Our prayer:

That you walk with God's face upon you,

Stepping out of cast shadows,

Into his light,

And that you hope,

Always and forever.

Amen and amen!

❀

The Hope Always Tool Kit

Dear brothers and sisters, one final thing.
Fix your thoughts on what is true, and honorable, and
right, and pure, and lovely, and admirable. Think about
things that are excellent and worthy of praise.

PHILIPPIANS 4:8

THIS TOOL KIT INCLUDES practical resources for you to reach people who are depressed and suicidal in your community. In it you will find:

- Twelve ways you can help save a life
- Lists of Scripture passages and quotes
- Playlists of uplifting hymns and songs
- Movies that can refill the well
- Fiction and nonfiction book recommendations
- A sample church policy
- Additional resources

If faith has helped you or a loved one overcome depression or suicide, I would like to hear your story! The same goes for churches that have started a suicide prevention initiative.

You can reach me at matthew@blessedearth.org. I hope to hear from you soon!

Twelve Ways You
Can Help Save a Life

HERE ARE TWELVE WAYS that you can encourage someone who is feeling depressed or suicidal. These ideas are things anyone can do to help.

1. **Visit.** People need to know that someone cares, and nothing shows that more than spending time together. Visit at their home or yours, at a restaurant or a coffee shop. Sit in a park or take a walk. There is no replacement for human touch, the human voice, and the presence of another person.

2. **Call.** A timely phone call and a listening ear can be lifesaving. If you don't know what to say, start with something like "I was thinking about you this morning and just wanted to check in and see how you are doing." Or "Is this an okay time to talk? I just wanted to tell you how much I love you and that I've been praying for you." No matter how you start, the important thing is to pay attention and listen.

3. **Ask questions.** Whether it's in person or over the phone, ask open-ended, nonjudgmental questions. Here are some examples:

    - "What are you doing for fun lately?"
    - "Are you getting outside?"

- "What music are you listening to?"
- "What does your routine look like these days?"
- "Are you having trouble sleeping?"
- "What was the high point and low point of the past week?"
- "On a scale of 1 to 10, how are you feeling today?"

The point is to get a fuller picture of their interior life and gently suggest ways to combat their despair.

4. **Send a passage from Scripture or an uplifting quote.** This can take many forms: emails, texts, handwritten notes on index cards, calligraphy posters, or even needlepoint. It can be quick and simple or framed and beautiful. A list of Scriptures and quotes to get you started is found in this tool kit (pages 174–191). Encourage your friend to claim God's Word as promises they can count on.

5. **Make a playlist or burn a CD of uplifting songs and hymns.** Music is one of the important ways many people hear the voice of God. As Dietrich Bonhoeffer once said, in times of care and sorrow, music "will keep a fountain of joy alive in you." This resource section includes a sampling of both Christian and secular music across the spectrum to get you started. Musical tastes vary; the important thing is to personalize the playlist for the individual you are trying to help.

6. **Write a letter and send it via snail mail.** In the age of electronic communication, receiving a card or letter in the mail is a special treat. The bonus is that the person can hold on to the letter and reread it when feeling despondent or hopeless.

7. **Share a prayer.** When my wife receives emails or texts asking for prayer, instead of responding with a promise, she sends a prayer right then and there. If you don't feel comfortable with unscripted prayer, you can send a few personalized lines followed by the Aaronic blessing:

The LORD bless thee, and keep thee:
The LORD make his face shine upon thee, and be gracious unto thee:
The LORD lift up his countenance upon thee, and give thee peace.

NUMBERS 6:24-26, KJV

8. **Share a meal.** More people than I can count have eaten around our table. Jesus did much of his teaching over shared meals for a reason: something about the relaxed environment helps people let down their guard and share what is really on their hearts. Your relationship is never the same once someone has been welcomed into your home. Note that the root of "hospitality" and "hospital" are the same; hospitality heals!

9. **Take a walk.** My wife keeps up with most of her friends on walk-talks. The lack of interruptions, the release of endorphins, the connection with God's creation, and the rhythm of walking side by side all help to build deeper connections. At the end, she holds hands and prays with the friend, reflecting what they have learned together and offering up any concerns to our Lord, the Great Healer.

10. **Sabbath together.** The Hebrew word for holy is *kadosh*, which means "set apart." Think of Sabbath time as a time set apart from worldly concerns, commerce, and work. If your friend has been withdrawing, ask them to join you for church or for a walk and a meal after worship. Or try practicing screenless Sundays together, a holy time set apart for family, friends, and God. It's been shown repeatedly that time spent in nature can be both uplifting and healing.

11. **Do something fun.** Sometimes just being together is more important than what you say. Play a board game, watch a movie, or listen to some favorite music together. Push back the furniture and dance. Read an uplifting fictional work or a book from the Bible aloud. Find a south-facing hill and soak up the sun. Go outside on a clear night and look at the stars. People who are depressed tend to isolate and turn inward. Jesus sought joy in community, and so should we.

12. **Get help.** One of the most important lessons I have learned is to know when I am in over my head. Don't try to do this alone. Often a person who is depressed doesn't have the energy to seek help. Or they might not have the clarity of mind to know where to begin looking. Having a couple of excellent Christian counselors that you can trust and can refer folks to is invaluable. Ask your pastor and friends for references so you are prepared when the need arises. Helping a person who is depressed can be taxing, so be sure you have people praying for an extra measure of strength, wisdom, and patience for you, too.

Scripture and Quotes:
Giving Voice to Our Pain

PEOPLE OFTEN FIND COMFORT in knowing that they are not alone in their pain. David, Solomon, Jonah, Elijah, Job, Jeremiah, and many other biblical characters experienced extreme depression, yet faith in God carried them through their darkest days. Even Jesus cried out to his Father. The bottom line: encourage your loved ones to share their pain with God and others. Voicing our pain is not only okay; it's a sign of strength and can be an important part of the healing process. The Scripture passages in this section will help them give voice to their pain and show them that they are not alone.

[Elijah] went on alone into the wilderness, traveling all day. He sat down under a solitary broom tree and prayed that he might die. "I have had enough, LORD," he said. "Take my life, for I am no better than my ancestors who have already died."

1 KINGS 19:4

Why wasn't I born dead?
    Why didn't I die as I came from the womb? . . .
I cannot eat for sighing;
    my groans pour out like water.

What I always feared has happened to me.
    What I dreaded has come true.
I have no peace, no quietness.
    I have no rest; only trouble comes.
JOB 3:11, 24-26

My God, my God, why have you abandoned me?
    Why are you so far away when I groan for help?
Every day I call to you, my God, but you do not answer.
    Every night I lift my voice, but I find no relief.
PSALM 22:1-2

I am poured out like water, and all my bones are out of joint: my
    heart is like wax; it is melted in the midst of my bowels.
My strength is dried up like a potsherd; and my tongue cleaveth to
    my jaws; and thou hast brought me into the dust of death.
PSALM 22:14-15, KJV

Day and night I have only tears for food,
    while my enemies continually taunt me, saying,
    "Where is this God of yours?"
PSALM 42:3

    Why have you tossed me aside?
Why must I wander around in grief, oppressed by my enemies? . . .
    O God, my God!
Why am I discouraged?
    Why is my heart so sad?
PSALM 43:2, 4-5

You have taken away my companions and loved ones.
    Darkness is my closest friend.
PSALM 88:18

I came to hate life because everything done here under the sun is so troubling. Everything is meaningless—like chasing the wind.

ECCLESIASTES 2:17

Oh, that I had died in my mother's womb,
    that her body had been my grave!
Why was I ever born?
    My entire life has been filled
    with trouble, sorrow, and shame.

JEREMIAH 20:17-18

Just kill me now, LORD! I'd rather be dead than alive.

JONAH 4:3

At about three o'clock, Jesus called out with a loud voice, *"Eli, Eli, lema sabachthani?"* which means "My God, my God, why have you abandoned me?"

MATTHEW 27:46

❋

It's not just biblical characters who suffer from depression and despair. Throughout history, countless people have expressed a desire to die yet have found the strength to face one more hour, one more day, and to go on to be a blessing to the world. Here are a few quotes that may help the people in your life who have lost hope to realize that they are not alone:

I am now the most miserable man living. If what I feel were equally distributed to the whole human family, there would not be one cheerful face on the earth. Whether I shall ever be better

I can not tell; I awfully forebode I shall not. To remain as I am is impossible; I must die or be better, it appears to me.

ABRAHAM LINCOLN,
LETTER TO FIRST LAW PARTNER JOHN T. STUART, 1841

I suppose some Brethren neither have much elevation or depression. I could almost wish to share their peaceful life, for I am much tossed up and down, and although my joy is greater than the most of men, my depression of spirit is such as few can have any idea of.

CHARLES SPURGEON,
ISRAEL'S GOD AND GOD'S ISRAEL, SERMON 803, 1868

I don't like standing near the edge of a platform when an express train is passing through. I like to stand right back and if possible to get a pillar between me and the train. I don't like to stand by the side of a ship and look down into the water. A second's action would end everything. A few drops of desperation.

WINSTON CHURCHILL,
DESCRIPTION OF THE "BLACK DOG" TO HIS PHYSICIAN,
LORD MORAN, 1944

Lord, my God, who am I that You should forsake me? The child of your love—and now become as the most hated one—the one You have thrown away as unwanted—unloved. I call, I cling, I want—and there is no One to answer—no One on Whom I can cling—no, No One.—Alone.

MOTHER TERESA,
LETTER TO FATHER PICACHY, 1959

Part of every misery is, so to speak, the misery's shadow or reflection: the fact that you don't merely suffer but have to keep on thinking about the fact that you suffer. I not only live each endless day in grief, but live each day thinking about living each day in grief.

C. S. LEWIS,
A GRIEF OBSERVED, 1961

To be in a state of depression is like that. It is to be unable to occupy yourself with anything much except your state of depression. Even the most marvelous thing is like music to the deaf. Even the greatest thing is like a shower of stars to the blind.

FREDERICK BUECHNER,
WHISTLING IN THE DARK, 1993

The anguish completely paralyzed me. I could no longer sleep. I cried uncontrollably for hours. I could not be reached by consoling words or arguments. I no longer had any interest in other people's problems. I lost all appetite for food and could not appreciate the beauty of music, art, or even nature. All had become darkness. Within me there was one long scream coming from a place I didn't know existed, a place full of demons.

HENRI NOUWEN,
THE INNER VOICE OF LOVE: A JOURNEY THROUGH ANGUISH TO FREEDOM,
PUBLISHED 1996

Scriptures and Quotes: Hope

GOD'S PROMISES are more powerful than our despair. He is always with us, even when we feel most alone. Below is a sampling of the many Scriptures you can send to loved ones who are feeling hopeless and helpless.

When Charles Spurgeon, who suffered from lifelong depression, was in a dark hole, he would look for a Scripture that exactly fit his need. He would then pray something like this: "Lord, this is your promise, and I have faith in your Word. I humbly plead for you to show me that this promise is true in my case."

A passage that Spurgeon turned to repeatedly was Psalm 103:13: "The LORD is like a father to his children, tender and compassionate to those who fear him." Spurgeon took God at his word and appealed for his Father's compassion to manifest itself in his life.

The righteous person faces many troubles,
   but the LORD comes to the rescue each time.

PSALM 34:19

He also turns deserts into pools of water,
   the dry land into springs of water.

PSALM 107:35

Restore our fortunes, LORD,
   as streams renew the desert.

Those who plant in tears
    will harvest with shouts of joy.
They weep as they go to plant their seed,
    but they sing as they return with the harvest.

PSALM 126:4-6

I will open up rivers for them on the high plateaus.
    I will give them fountains of water in the valleys.
I will fill the desert with pools of water.
    Rivers fed by springs will flow across the parched ground.

ISAIAH 41:18

God, the LORD, created the heavens and stretched them out.
    He created the earth and everything in it.
He gives breath to everyone,
    life to everyone who walks the earth.

ISAIAH 42:5

I will brighten the darkness before them
    and smooth out the road ahead of them.
Yes, I will indeed do these things;
    I will not forsake them.

ISAIAH 42:16

Do not be afraid, for I have ransomed you.
    I have called you by name; you are mine.
When you go through deep waters,
    I will be with you.
When you go through rivers of difficulty,
    you will not drown.
When you walk through the fire of oppression,
    you will not be burned up;
        the flames will not consume you.

ISAIAH 43:1-2

Do not be afraid, for I am with you.

ISAIAH 43:5

From eternity to eternity I am God.
    No one can snatch anyone out of my hand.
    No one can undo what I have done.

ISAIAH 43:13

I am about to do something new.
    See, I have already begun! Do you not see it?
I will make a pathway through the wilderness.
    I will create rivers in the dry wasteland.

ISAIAH 43:19

I have swept away your sins like a cloud.
    I have scattered your offenses like the morning mist.
Oh, return to me,
    for I have paid the price to set you free.

ISAIAH 44:22

I am the LORD your God,
    who teaches you what is good for you
    and leads you along the paths you should follow.

ISAIAH 48:17

Can a mother forget her nursing child?
    Can she feel no love for the child she has borne?
But even if that were possible,
    I would not forget you!
See, I have written your name on the palms of my hands.

ISAIAH 49:15-16

Who among you fears the LORD
    and obeys his servant?

If you are walking in darkness,
    without a ray of light,
trust in the LORD
    and rely on your God.

ISAIAH 50:10

"The mountains may move
    and the hills disappear,
but even then my faithful love for you will remain.
    My covenant of blessing will never be broken,"
    says the LORD, who has mercy on you.

ISAIAH 54:10

Seek the LORD while you can find him.
    Call on him now while he is near.

ISAIAH 55:6

You will live in joy and peace.
    The mountains and hills will burst into song,
    and the trees of the field will clap their hands!

ISAIAH 55:12

I restore the crushed spirit of the humble
    and revive the courage of those with repentant hearts.

ISAIAH 57:15

The LORD will guide you continually,
    giving you water when you are dry
    and restoring your strength.
You will be like a well-watered garden,
    like an ever-flowing spring.

ISAIAH 58:11

Listen! The LORD's arm is not too weak to save you,
    nor is his ear too deaf to hear you call.

ISAIAH 59:1

Darkness as black as night covers all the nations of the earth,
    but the glory of the LORD rises and appears over you.

ISAIAH 60:2

The Spirit of the Sovereign LORD is upon me,
    for the LORD has anointed me
    to bring good news to the poor.
He has sent me to comfort the brokenhearted
    and to proclaim that captives will be released
    and prisoners will be freed.

ISAIAH 61:1

For since the world began,
    no ear has heard
and no eye has seen a God like you,
    who works for those who wait for him!

ISAIAH 64:4

I will answer them before they even call to me.
    While they are still talking about their needs,
    I will go ahead and answer their prayers!

ISAIAH 65:24

Blessed are those who trust in the LORD
    and have made the LORD their hope and confidence.
They are like trees planted along a riverbank,
    with roots that reach deep into the water.
Such trees are not bothered by the heat
    or worried by long months of drought.

Their leaves stay green,
　　and they never stop producing fruit.

JEREMIAH 17:7-8

"For I know the plans I have for you," says the LORD. "They are plans for good and not for disaster, to give you a future and a hope."

JEREMIAH 29:11

Tears of joy will stream down their faces,
　　and I will lead them home with great care.
They will walk beside quiet streams
　　and on smooth paths where they will not stumble.

JEREMIAH 31:9

I will turn their mourning into joy.
　　I will comfort them and exchange their sorrow for rejoicing.

JEREMIAH 31:13

What is the price of two sparrows—one copper coin? But not a single sparrow can fall to the ground without your Father knowing it. And the very hairs on your head are all numbered. So don't be afraid; you are more valuable to God than a whole flock of sparrows.

MATTHEW 10:29-31

Anyone who believes in me may come and drink! For the Scriptures declare, "Rivers of living water will flow from his heart."

JOHN 7:38

I have told you all this so that you may have peace in me. Here on earth you will have many trials and sorrows. But take heart, because I have overcome the world.

JOHN 16:33

We can rejoice, too, when we run into problems and trials, for we know that they help us develop endurance. And endurance develops strength of character, and character strengthens our confident hope of salvation.

ROMANS 5:3-4

Yet what we suffer now is nothing compared to the glory he will reveal to us later.

ROMANS 8:18

If God is for us, who can ever be against us? Since he did not spare even his own Son but gave him up for us all, won't he also give us everything else?

ROMANS 8:31-32

Can anything ever separate us from Christ's love? Does it mean he no longer loves us if we have trouble or calamity, or are persecuted, or hungry, or destitute, or in danger, or threatened with death? . . . No, despite all these things, overwhelming victory is ours through Christ, who loved us.

ROMANS 8:35, 37

He comforts us in all our troubles so that we can comfort others. When they are troubled, we will be able to give them the same comfort God has given us.

2 CORINTHIANS 1:4

We are pressed on every side by troubles, but we are not crushed. We are perplexed, but not driven to despair. We are hunted down, but never abandoned by God. We get knocked down, but we are not destroyed.

2 CORINTHIANS 4:8-9

Our present troubles are small and won't last very long. Yet they produce for us a glory that vastly outweighs them and will last forever!

2 CORINTHIANS 4:17-18

Take a new grip with your tired hands and strengthen your weak knees. Mark out a straight path for your feet so that those who are weak and lame will not fall but become strong.

HEBREWS 12:12-13

Dear brothers and sisters, when troubles of any kind come your way, consider it an opportunity for great joy. For you know that when your faith is tested, your endurance has a chance to grow.

JAMES 1:2-3

God blesses those who patiently endure testing and temptation. Afterward they will receive the crown of life that God has promised to those who love him.

JAMES 1:12

Come close to God, and God will come close to you.

JAMES 4:8

Give all your worries and cares to God, for he cares about you.

1 PETER 5:7

Don't worry about anything; instead, pray about everything. Tell God what you need, and thank him for all he has done. Then you will experience God's peace, which exceeds anything we can understand. His peace will guard your hearts and minds as you live in Christ Jesus.

PHILIPPIANS 4:6-7

He will lead them to springs of life-giving water. And God will wipe every tear from their eyes.

REVELATION 7:17

He will wipe every tear from their eyes, and there will be no more death or sorrow or crying or pain. All these things are gone forever.

REVELATION 21:4

❋

Your loved one may also be inspired by quotes from people through the ages who have experienced pain and suffering and yet endured. Below are some uplifting quotes to share with loved ones:

In my deepest wound I saw your glory, and it astounded me.

AUGUSTINE (354–430)

God loves each of us as if there were only one of us.

AUGUSTINE (354–430)

We are saved by faith alone, but the faith that saves is never alone.

MARTIN LUTHER (1483–1546)

So when the devil throws your sins in your face and declares that you deserve death and hell, tell him this: "I admit that I deserve death and hell, what of it? For I know One who suffered and made satisfaction on my behalf. His name is Jesus Christ, Son of God, and where He is there I shall be also!"

MARTIN LUTHER (1483–1546)

Our righteousness is in Him, and our hope depends, not upon the exercise of grace in us, but upon the fullness of grace and love in Him and upon His obedience unto death.

JOHN NEWTON (1725–1807)

Remember, in the depth and even agony of despondency, that very shortly you are to feel well again.

ABRAHAM LINCOLN (1809–1865)

Hope is the thing with feathers that perches in the soul and sings the tune without the words—And never stops at all.

EMILY DICKINSON (1830–1886)

All our infirmities, whatever they are, are just opportunities for God to display his gracious work in us.

CHARLES SPURGEON (1834–1892)

I know, perhaps as well as anyone, what depression means, and what it is to feel myself sinking lower and lower. Yet at the worst, when I reach the lowest depths, I have an inward peace which no pain or depression can in the least disturb. Trusting in Jesus Christ my Savior, there is still a blessed quietness in the deep caverns of my soul, though upon the surface, a rough tempest may be raging, and there may be little apparent calm.

CHARLES SPURGEON (1834–1892)

I note that some whom I greatly love and esteem, who are, in my judgment among the very choicest of God's people, nevertheless, travel most of the way to heaven by night.

CHARLES SPURGEON (1834–1892)

No sin is necessarily connected with sorrow of heart, for Jesus Christ our Lord once said, "My soul is exceeding sorrowful even unto death." There was no sin in him, and consequently none in his deep depression.

CHARLES SPURGEON (1834–1892)

The iron bolt which so mysteriously fastens the door of hope and holds our spirits in gloomy prison, needs a heavenly hand to push it back.

CHARLES SPURGEON (1834–1892)

Let this one great, gracious, glorious fact lie in your spirit until it perfumes all your thoughts and makes you rejoice even though you are without strength, seeing the Lord Jesus has become your strength and your song, yes, He has become your salvation.

CHARLES SPURGEON (1834–1892)

The other gods were strong, but Thou wast weak
They rode, but Thou didst stumble to a throne
But to our wounds only God's wounds can speak
And not a god has wounds, but Thou alone.

EDWARD SHILLITO (1872–1948)

Remember Whose you are and Whom you serve. Provoke yourself by recollection, and your affection for God will increase tenfold; your imagination will not be starved any longer, but will be quick and enthusiastic, and your hope will be inexpressibly bright.

OSWALD CHAMBERS (1874–1917)

Hope means hoping when things are hopeless, or it is no virtue at all. . . . As long as matters are really hopeful, hope is a mere flattery or platitude; it is only when everything is hopeless that hope begins to be a strength.

G. K. CHESTERTON (1874–1936)

Our world today desperately hungers for hope, and yet uncounted people have almost given up. There is despair and hopelessness on every hand. Let us be faithful in proclaiming the hope that is in Jesus!

BILLY GRAHAM (1918–2018)

Death is not a period that ends the great sentence of life, but a comma that punctuates it to a more lofty significance. Death is not a blind alley that leads the human race into a state of nothingness, but an open door which leads man into eternal life.

MARTIN LUTHER KING JR. (1929–1968)

Genuine self-acceptance is not derived from the power of positive thinking, mind games, or pop psychology. *It is an act of faith* in the God of grace.

BRENNAN MANNING (1934–2013)

Hope is called the anchor of the soul (Hebrews 6:19), because it gives stability to the Christian life. But hope is not simply a "wish" (I wish that such-and-such would take place); rather, it is that which latches on to the certainty of the promises of the future that God has made.

R. C. SPROUL (1939–2017)

The best we can hope for in this life is a knothole peek at the shining realities ahead. Yet a glimpse is enough. It's enough to convince our hearts that whatever sufferings and sorrows currently assail us aren't worthy of comparison to that which waits over the horizon.

JONI EARECKSON TADA (1949–)

Suffering is at the very heart of the Christian faith. It is not only the way Christ became like and redeemed us, but it is one of the main ways we become like him and experience his redemption. And that means that our suffering, despite its painfulness, is also filled with purpose and usefulness.

TIMOTHY KELLER (1950–)

If you remember with grateful amazement that Jesus was thrown into the ultimate furnace *for* you, you can begin to sense him in your smaller furnaces *with* you.

TIMOTHY KELLER (1950–)

As a man who seemed about to lose both his career and his family once said to me, "I always knew, in principle, that 'Jesus is all you need' to get through. But you don't really know Jesus is all you need until Jesus is all you have."

TIMOTHY KELLER (1950–)

People with depression have something very valuable to teach us—how to live when it doesn't ever feel good.

KAY WARREN (1954–)

The church needs to value and recognize the incredible courage of those struggling with mental illness.

KAY WARREN (1954–)

If my liver doesn't work perfectly and I take a pill for that, there's no shame in that. Why is it that if my brain doesn't work perfectly and I take a pill I'm supposed to hide that?

RICK WARREN (1954–)

Hymns and Songs to Uplift

Who hears music, feels his solitude peopled at once.

ROBERT BROWNING

I HAVE LOVED MUSIC FOREVER. My tastes range from classical to electronic to rock and roll. Music has been my comforter in times of trouble, my solace while studying, and my tether to God when feeling most alone. Below are a few of the songs I can count on to lift me up:

- Handel's *Messiah* (I particularly love Christopher Hogwood and The Academy of Ancient Music's version)
- *The Four Seasons* (Vivaldi)
- *Brandenburg Concertos* (Bach)
- "The Hills of Home" (Kevin Braheny and Tim Clark—I was an early fan of electronic and minimalist music and started listening to it in undergraduate school. Some of my favorite artists include Tetsu Inoue, Solar Quest, Michael Hedges, and John Adams)
- "Hold It Up to the Light" (David Wilcox)
- "God Is Love" (Marvin Gaye)
- "Love Is the Key" (Tuck & Patti)
- "I Hope You Dance" (Lee Ann Womack)
- "Cornerstone" (Hillsong)
- "I Will Move on Up a Little Higher" (Mahalia Jackson)
- "People Get Ready" (Eva Cassidy)

I asked a number of friends to recommend songs that lift them up when they're feeling down, and the following lists are the result.

MODERN WORSHIP SONGS
- "As the Deer" (written by Martin Nystrom)
- "Blessed Be Your Name" (Matt Redman)
- "Come as You Are" (David Crowder)
- "Eye of the Storm" (Ryan Stevenson)
- "The Father's House" (Cory Asbury)
- "His Eye Is on the Sparrow" (Lauryn Hill and Tanya Blount)
- "How Deep the Father's Love for Us" (Stuart Townend)
- "I Can Only Imagine" (MercyMe)
- "In Christ Alone" (Stuart Townend)
- "Join the Triumph" (Citizens & Saints)
- "O Church, Arise" (Keith and Kristyn Getty)
- "O Come to the Altar" (Elevation Worship)
- Psalms (John Michael Talbot)
- "Remind Me Who I Am" (Jason Gray)
- "Surrounded (Fight My Battles)" (Michael W. Smith)
- "To God All Praise and Glory" (The Sing Team)
- "Together" (For King and Country)
- "Who You Say I Am" (Hillsong)
- "Your Great Name" (Natalie Grant)

TRADITIONAL HYMNS TO UPLIFT
- "All Creatures of Our God and King"
- "Amazing Grace"
- "Be Thou My Vision"
- "Because He Lives"
- "Blessed Assurance, Jesus Is Mine"
- "Come, Thou Fount of Every Blessing"
- "For the Beauty of the Earth"

- "Great Is Thy Faithfulness"
- "Holy, Holy, Holy"
- "How Great Thou Art"
- "It Is Well with My Soul"
- "A Mighty Fortress Is Our God"
- "Ode to Joy"
- "Rock of Ages"
- "Turn Your Eyes upon Jesus"

OTHER RECOMMENDATIONS
- "Amazing Day" (Coldplay)
- "Cups (D'ror Yikra)" (Maccabeats)
- "Drawn to You" (Audrey Assad)
- "Fireflies" (Owl City)
- "Good Shabbos" (Six13)
- "Heaven Is Around Us" (Stu Garrard feat. John Mark McMillan)
- "Heavy" (Birdtalker)
- "I Can See Clearly Now" (Jimmy Cliff)
- "Lay It Down" (Matt Maher)
- "Meant to Live" (Switchfoot)
- "Pilgrim" (John Mark McMillan)
- "Selah III (Fruits of the Spirit)" (Hillsong Young and Free)
- "Sheep May Safely Graze," BWV 208 (Bach)
- "Suite for Orchestra No. 3 in D Major," BWV 1068: II. Air (Bach)
- "The Sun Is Shining" (Third Day)
- "To My Knees (Live)" (Hillsong Young and Free)
- "The Valley Song (Sing of Your Mercy)" (Jars of Clay)
- "What a Wonderful World" (Louis Armstrong)
- "Where the Streets Have No Name" (U2)

Movies to Uplift

BELOW ARE SOME MOVIE RECOMMENDATIONS that you might want to watch together with a loved one. Most of these movies are uplifting and inspirational, with good triumphing over evil. They all have a hero or someone who learns important lessons that help them overcome the problems they face. Next to each movie is an age recommendation so you can determine if it's okay for family members to join you; please screen before sharing with a young friend, and use your best judgment based on the individual circumstances. (Most age suggestions are from Common Sense Media.)

- *The Adventures of Milo and Otis* (1986, 5+)
- *Kiki's Delivery Service* (1989, 5+)
- *My Neighbor Totoro* (1988, 5+)
- *Homeward Bound* (1993, 6+)
- *Inside Out* (2015, 6+)
- *Ratatouille* (2007, 6+)
- *Up* (2009, 6+)
- *Batkid Begins* (2015, 7+)
- *Akeelah and the Bee* (2006, 8+)
- *Anne of Green Gables* (1985, 8+)
- *Fly Away Home* (1996, 8+)

- *Galaxy Quest* (1999, 8+)
- *The Princess Bride* (1987, 8+)
- *The Chronicles of Narnia: The Lion, the Witch, and the Wardrobe* (2005, 9+)
- *It's a Wonderful Life* (1946, 9+)
- *Spirited Away* (2001, 9+)
- *Back to the Future* (1985, 10+)
- *A Beautiful Day in the Neighborhood* (2019, 10+)
- *I Can Only Imagine* (2018, 10+)
- *Newsies* (1992, 9+)
- *October Sky* (1999, 10+)
- *Queen of Katwe* (2016, 10+)
- *Won't You Be My Neighbor?* (2018, 10+)
- *Chariots of Fire* (1981, 11+)
- *Groundhog Day* (1993, 11+)
- *Little Women* (1994, 11+)
- *Pride and Prejudice* (1995, 11+)
- *The Robe* (1953, 11+)
- *Sense and Sensibility* (1995, 11+)
- *The Wind Rises* (2013, 11+)
- *The Boy Who Harnessed the Wind* (2019, 12+)
- *Cranford* (2007, 12+)
- *The Guernsey Literary and Potato Peel Pie Society* (2018, 12+)
- *North and South* (2004, 12+)
- *We Bought a Zoo* (2011, 12+)
- *Wives and Daughters* (1999, 12+)
- *Mansfield Park* (1999, 13+)

Books to Uplift

WITHOUT BOOKS, I'D BE LOST. Obviously, *the* Book should be a staple in anyone's reading. Consider this a beginning list of supplemental texts. These books have helped me (or some of my friends) through difficult seasons, providing inspiration and hope when all seemed dark and lost. Again, before recommending a book to a friend or giving them a copy as a gift, please read it yourself.

FICTION
- *All Creatures Great and Small* (James Herriot)
- *Anne of Green Gables* (L. M. Montgomery)
- *At the Back of the North Wind* (George MacDonald)
- *A Chameleon, a Boy, and a Quest* (J. A. Myhre)
- *A Christmas Carol* (Charles Dickens)
- *The Country of the Pointed Firs* (Sarah Orne Jewett)
- The Chronicles of Narnia (C. S. Lewis)
- *Cranford* (Elizabeth Gaskell)
- *Freckles* (Gene Stratton-Porter)
- *Frog and Toad Are Friends* (Arnold Lobel) ✓
- *A Girl of the Limberlost* (Gene Stratton-Porter)
- *The Great Divorce* (C. S. Lewis)

- *Heidi* (Johanna Spyri)
- *The Hobbit* and The Lord of the Rings trilogy (J. R. R. Tolkien)
- *Les Misérables* (Victor Hugo)
- *The Little Engine That Could* (Watty Piper) ✓
- *A Little Princess* (Frances Hodgson Burnett)
- *Little Women* (Louisa May Alcott)
- *Mansfield Park* (Jane Austen)
- *Oh, the Places You'll Go* (Dr. Seuss) ✓
- "Perfection" and "Monday" (Mark Helprin—short stories in *The Pacific and Other Stories*)
- *The Screwtape Letters* (C. S. Lewis)
- *The Secret Garden* (Frances Hodgson Burnett)
- *Silas Marner* (George Eliot)
- *Stepping Heavenward* (Elizabeth Payson Prentiss)
- Swallows and Amazons series (Arthur Ransome)
- *Tom Brown's Schooldays* (Thomas Hughes)
- *The Trumpet of the Swan* (E. B. White) ✓
- *Winnie the Pooh* (A. A. Milne)
- *A Wrinkle in Time* (Madeleine L'Engle)

NONFICTION

- *And There Was Light: The Extraordinary Memoir of a Blind Hero of the French Resistance in World War II* (Jacques Lusseyran)
- *For the Glory: The Untold and Inspiring Story of Eric Liddell, Hero of Chariots of Fire* (Duncan Hamilton)
- *God in You: A Conversation* (John Stumbo)
- *Hinds' Feet on High Places* (Hannah Hurnard)
- *I Bought a House on Gratitude Street: And Other Insights on the Good Life* (or anything by J. Ellsworth Kalas)
- *Life of the Beloved: Spiritual Living in a Secular World* (Henri Nouwen)
- *One Man's Meat* (E. B. White)

- *The Problem of Pain* (really, anything by C. S. Lewis)
- *The Promise: God Works All Things Together for Your Good* (Robert Morgan)
- *The Red Sea Rules: The Same God Who Led You in Will Lead You Out* (Robert Morgan)
- *Spurgeon's Sorrows: Realistic Hope for Those Who Suffer from Depression* (Zack Eswine)
- *The Strength You Need: The Twelve Great Strength Passages of the Bible* (Robert Morgan)
- *Then Sings My Soul: 150 of the World's Greatest Hymn Stories* (Robert Morgan)
- *Unbroken: A World War II Story of Survival, Resilience, and Redemption* (Laura Hillenbrand)
- *Walking with God through Pain and Suffering* (Timothy Keller)
- *Walking with Henry: Big Lessons from a Little Donkey on Faith, Friendship, and Finding Your Path* (Rachel Anne Ridge)
- *When the Bottom Drops Out: Finding Grace in the Depths of Disappointment* (Robert Bugh)

Sample Suicide Prevention Church Policy

BELOW IS A SAMPLE POLICY that you can adapt for your church.[1] Before including this or a similar policy in your church policy manual, we recommend seeking legal review and advice.

If a leader learns of an individual considering suicide or talking about self-harm, they are to contact _____ for instructions on how to proceed. If _____ cannot be reached immediately or the concern appears to be an emergency, immediately contact 911. Stay with the person until help arrives.

Below are five things to do before the individual leaves. If they do leave before you are able to have a full conversation with them, contact 911 immediately.

1. **Ask them the tough questions.** Asking them if they are suicidal will not give them the idea or make them stop talking to you. Here are some ways you can ask:
   - Are you having any thoughts of harming yourself?
   - Do you ever wish you could go to sleep and never wake up?

2. **Recognize the limits of confidentiality.** If they ask you to keep your conversation secret, your response needs to be, "I know this is hard to talk about, but I can't make any promises until I know you are safe."

3. **Start a support network with others.** Connect them with someone they feel safe to talk with about their suicidal thoughts. If they are under the age of eighteen, you must inform their legal guardian(s). When you find someone to talk with them, make sure they are a good fit and that they understand what you are asking of them. Get them to confirm they are willing to do it.

4. **Ask if they have professional counseling.** Ask if the individual is already in counseling, and if they are, get the name and phone number of the person they are seeing. If a person is talking about self-harm and/or suicidal ideation, there is a need for therapy. We encourage church leadership and congregation members to take the role of support and refer this person to a licensed professional counselor to do mental health treatment. Counselors are bound to HIPAA, so make sure as the lead support from the church for this individual, you ask the parent or individual (if they are over the age of eighteen) to sign a release so you can check how you can support the person.

5. **Do not leave a person at imminent risk of suicide alone.** If you have any suspicions that a person is seriously considering harming themselves, let the person know that you care, that he or she is not alone, and that you are there to help. You may have to work with the person's family to ensure that he or she will be adequately supported until a mental health professional can provide an assessment. In some cases, you may have to accompany the person to the emergency room at an area hospital or crisis center. If the person is uncooperative, combative, or otherwise unwilling to seek help, and if you sense that the person is in acute danger, call 911. Tell the dispatcher that you are concerned that the person with you "is a danger to himself/herself" or "cannot take care of himself/herself." These key phrases will alert the dispatcher to locate immediate care for this person with the help of police. Do not hesitate to make such a call if you suspect that someone may be a danger to himself or herself. It could save that person's life.

Below are some additional guidelines that come from the Suicide Prevention Lifeline:

- **Take your loved one seriously:** Some people feel that kids who say they are going to hurt or kill themselves are "just doing it for attention." But if your child, friend, or family member confides thoughts of suicide, believe them and get help.

- **Listen with empathy and provide support:** A fight or breakup might not seem like a big deal, but for a young person it can feel immense. Sympathize and listen. Minimizing what your child or friend is going through can increase his or her sense of hopelessness.

- **Learn the warning signs:** Friends sometimes let friends know if they are thinking about suicide or dying. Other times, changes in behavior may show that someone is struggling.

- **Don't keep suicide a secret:** If your friend is considering suicide, don't promise to keep it a secret. Tell him or her you can help, but you need to involve other people, like a trusted adult. Neither of you have to face this alone.[2]

Make sure you have the following resources always available to give out to people:

National Suicide Prevention Lifeline
1-800-273-8255
https://suicidepreventionlifeline.org/
The Lifeline on Twitter: @800273TALK
(https://twitter.com/800273TALK)

Additional Resources

What do we live for, if it is not to make life less difficult to each other?

GEORGE ELIOT

National Suicide Prevention Lifeline (1-800-273-TALK [8255]): The national hotline to call if someone you love is suicidal.

Celebrate Recovery (celebraterecovery.com): A Christ-centered, 12-step recovery program for anyone struggling with hurt, pain, or addiction of any kind.

Fresh Hope (freshhope.us): An international network of Christian support groups for those who have a mental health diagnosis and for their loved ones.

Soul Shop (soulshopmovement.org): An organization that helps train and equip churches and Christian leaders to address depression and suicide in their communities.

Remedy Live (remedylive.com): A ministry that supports people with depression, suicidal ideation, and other mental health issues through live chat and text chat.

Alcoholics Anonymous (aa.org): An international fellowship of men and women who have had a drinking problem. Membership is open to anyone who wants to do something about his or her drinking problem through a 12-step program.

Narcotics Anonymous (na.org): An international fellowship of men and women who have had a drug problem. Membership is open to anyone who wants to do something about his or her drug problem through a 12-step program.

Al-Anon Family Groups (al-anon.org): A mutual support program for people whose lives have been affected by someone else's drinking.

Mental Health: A Guide for Faith Leaders and *Quick Reference on Mental Health for Faith Leaders* (psychiatry.org): Designed for pastors and lay leaders, this is a concise, practical overview on how to approach mental health in the church setting.[3]

Brief Cognitive Behavioral Therapy for Suicide Prevention, Craig J. Bryan and M. David Rudd (New York: Guildford Press, 2018): While primarily written for clinicians, this book also provides practical tools that can be adapted for churches and individuals supporting a loved one in crisis, including reproducible handouts on possible warning signs, a crisis support plan, healthy sleep hygiene, and common self-management strategies.

Discussion Guide

1. How has suicide touched you? What objects in your life are "haunted" the way the author describes (see page 1)?

2. In his tale of two patients, the author shows the difference that faith makes in the life of one person. How does faith play a protective role when it comes to suicide? How do other avenues to finding meaning in life fall short?

3. In chapter 2, the author examines the extent of the suicide crisis and why current statistics do not accurately represent the problem. Are the numbers or the extent of the problem surprising to you? Explain.

4. The author predicts that "if we continue on the current path, society will ultimately normalize suicide" (pages 31–32). How would you respond to someone who believes that suicide is not morally wrong but a "life choice"?

5. The right side of the Life Continuum Scale represents people who are focused on others in life-giving ways. The left side describes individuals who are self-focused and demonstrate attitudes and behaviors that are life taking. Is there someone you are concerned about who is traveling down the left side of the continuum? How far to the left side do you think that person is, and why? How might you help them move right on the continuum?

6. In chapter 4, the author gives an overview of various mental illnesses that are often associated with depression and suicidal ideation. In your view, what is the role of mental health professionals in caring for people who may have a mental disorder? If you are a pastor or church worker, when is it appropriate to refer someone in your care to a mental health professional?

7. "Unlike every other creature on earth, we are drawn toward things that we know will harm us. . . . God is light and truth. Satan represents death and lies" (page 72). What are some of the lies people believe that lead to self-harm? What are truths about God that combat these lies?

8. After a great victory against the prophets of Baal, the prophet Elijah feared for his life and fled into the wilderness. At his lowest point he told God he wanted to die (see 1 Kings 18–19). What does Elijah's despair tell us about human vulnerability? What can we learn from the way God met Elijah's physical needs? What restored Elijah's hope and will to live?

9. How did Jesus show love and compassion to people with mental illness and those possessed by demons? Consider Luke 8:26-33 (page 95). We may be tempted to judge or give up on such people today. How does this story influence the way you view people who suffer in this way?

10. The author reports that "50 to 70 percent of those who commit suicide have drugs or alcohol in their system" (page 101). He writes that 12-step programs are the most effective treatment for alcoholism. What help in your area can you recommend for someone struggling with drug or alcohol addiction? How can you become better prepared to support a recovering alcoholic or drug addict?

11. The author suggests memorizing three questions to ask to determine if a person is in imminent danger of suicide. Review these questions on pages 122–124 and the follow-up steps to take if necessary. With a partner, role play a conversation in which you practice asking these questions gently yet directly (or imagine or write down a practice conversation). How can you demonstrate that you care as you listen and invite honest responses?

12. The mnemonic SIG E CAPS is a tool professionals use to screen for depression. It stands for sleep, interest, guilt, energy, concentration, appetite, psychomotor, and suicidal ideation. In chapter 8, the author suggests using this tool to help a loved one by looking for causes of depression and offers practical suggestions of ways to help. Which of his suggestions can you implement with a friend or loved one now? What other ideas would you add to the list? What helps you the most when you are feeling down?

13. The author writes, "When it comes to suicide, we are all living on the coast. Every Christian needs to be prepared to help save a friend who is over their head in the sea of depression" (page 142). What are the three most important things you have learned in this book that you will implement to help a friend in this state?

14. Pastors are not immune to depression and suicide, and church history offers examples of preachers, such as Charles Spurgeon, who had dark seasons of depression. How can you support clergy who are prone to depression? If you are a pastor who struggles with depression, what help are you actively pursuing?

15. What training can your church provide to lay leaders to help them recognize when a person may be suicidal and take appropriate steps to support them?

16. What new ministries might your church consider starting to offer hope and help to people who are depressed or suicidal? How can your church support those who have family members with mental illness? How can you foster a church culture that shows compassion to hurting people and invites open conversations about depression and suicide?

17. The Hope Always Tool Kit on page 169 provides practical resources to use in helping people who are depressed or suicidal. What additional resources would you add to the lists in the tool kit?

18. Ask God to show you who in your life needs encouragement and comfort. How can you show them today that you care? In what ways can you bring the hope of Christ to them?

Notes

INTRODUCTION
1. See Matthew 15:14.

CHAPTER 1: A TALE OF TWO PATIENTS
1. Another interesting place we see this is at the beginning of Genesis 5. We find this eerie line of what could only be described as science fiction—until modern science came into being: "This is the book of the generations of Adam. When God created man, he made him in the likeness of God. Male and female he created them, and blessed them and named them Man when they were created" (Genesis 5:1-2, ESV). Although this phrasing ("named them Man") is written out of many modern Bible translations, I promise it is there in the original Hebrew manuscripts. What is so amazing about this account of men and women being made in the image of God and God calling them *Man*? I don't think it has anything to do with the greater or lesser status of one or the other sex (presumably the rationale behind modern translators redacting it)—the verse makes it exquisitely clear that *both* men and women are made in God's image. Rather, the line was written by the one who invented our genetic code. It's how I would put it if I had to write an account that had to make it through five thousand years of copying and translation into various languages and across vast changes in human technology and scientific understanding. Both women (X, X chromosomes only) and men (X and Y chromosomes) are made in God's image, but only males carry the complete (determinate) chromosomes for both sexes. In other words, males carry both kinds of chromosomes that make up all humanity. God designed humanity very carefully, and modern genetics verifies what the Bible said thousands of years before. Again, we are not an accident!
2. Caitlyn Johnson, "Cutting through Advertising Clutter," *CBS*, September 17, 2006, https://www.cbsnews.com/news/cutting-through-advertising-clutter/; Neil Patel, "Which U.S. Brands Are Spending the Most on Advertising?" (blog), accessed September 23, 2020, https://neilpatel.com/blog/top-ad-spenders/; Erica Sweeney, "Kantar: US Ad Spend Reached $151B in 2018, a 4.1% Jump," *Marketing Dive*, January 24, 2019, https://www.marketingdive.com/news/kantar-us-ad-spend -reached-151b-in-2018-a-41-jump/546725/.

3. "Teens Are Spending Nearly Half Their Waking Hours on Screens—and That Can Have Scary, Lasting Effects," *MarketWatch*, October 28, 2019, https://www .marketwatch.com/story/the-scary-lasting-effects-of-too-much-screen-time-on-children-2019-04-10#:~:text=Children%20ages%208%20to%2012,habits%20 and%20rates%20programming%20for; "Violence in the Media and Entertainment (Position Paper)," American Academy of Family Practice, https://www.aafp.org /about/policies/all/violence-media-entertainment.html; "The Nielsen Total Audience Report: August 2020," August 13, 2020, https://www.nielsen.com/us/en /insights/report/2020/the-nielsen-total-audience-report-august-2020/; John Koblin, "How Much Do We Love TV? Let Us Count the Ways," *New York Times*, June 30, 2016, https://www.nytimes.com/2016/07/01/business/media/nielsen-survey-media -viewing.html; J. Clement, "Daily Social Media Usage Worldwide 2012–2019," Statista, February 26, 2020, https://www.statista.com/statistics/433871/daily-social -media-usage-worldwide/; Center on Media and Child Health, "Video Games," accessed October 28, 2020, http://cmch.tv/parents/video-games/.
4. Andrew Wu, Jing-Yu Wang, and Cun-Xian Jia, "Religion and Completed Suicide: A Meta-Analysis," *PLOS ONE*, June 25, 2015, https://journals.plos.org/plosone /article?id=10.1371/journal.pone.0131715; Robin Edward Gearing and Dana Alonzo, "Religion and Suicide: New Findings," *Journal of Religion and Health*, May 7, 2018, https://link.springer.com/article/10.1007/s10943-018-0629-8; B. H. Amit et al., "Religiosity Is a Protective Factor against Self-Injurious Thoughts and Behaviors in Jewish Adolescents: Findings from a Nationally Representative Survey," *European Psychiatry* 29, no. 8, October 2014, 509–513, https://www.cambridge .org/core/journals/european-psychiatry/article/religiosity-is-a-protective-factor -against-selfinjurious-thoughts-and-behaviors-in-jewish-adolescents-findings-from -a-nationally-representative-survey/218CA060F8420EF6B63EAD5AA5BD7096#.

CHAPTER 2: THE GREATEST DEPRESSION

1. At the height of the Great Depression, in 1932, the suicide rate was 21.9 suicides per 100,000 people, and it fell to 14 per 100,000 by 1942. As we will see in the following sections, even compared to the rate at the peak of the Great Depression, our suicide crisis today is much, much worse. In medical school, professors frequently offered the sage advice, "If you read different books, they say different things." The person I sat beside in lectures put this quote on the front of her notebook. Every time a professor said this line, she'd flip to the front of her notebook and circle it. At the end of the semester, it looked like a spirograph drawing. Statistics vary on suicide in the Great Depression through our present time. I studied actuary tables and have used conservative figures. The exact numbers aren't really our concern here. Trends are. And all agree on the point I am making: suicide rates are climbing greatly, and they would be much worse if modern medicine did not intervene.
2. "Suicide Statistics," American Foundation for Suicide Prevention, accessed September 23, 2020, https://afsp.org/suicide-statistics/.
3. Lea Winerman, "By the Numbers: Antidepressant Use on the Rise," *Monitor on*

Psychology 48, no. 10 (November 2017): 120, https://www.apa.org/monitor /2017/11/numbers; Kirsten Weir, "Worrying Trends in U.S. Suicide Rates," *Monitor on Psychology* 50, no. 3 (March 2019): 24, https://www.apa.org/monitor/2019/03 /trends-suicide.

4. Caitlyn Shelton, "Feeling the Pressures of the Pandemic: Suicide Hotlines See 800 Percent Spike in Calls," Fox 17 WZTV Nashville, April 14, 2020, https://fox17 .com/news/local/feeling-the-pressures-of-the-pandemic-suicide-hotlines-see-800 -percent-spike-in-calls; Mark É. Czeisler et al., "Mental Health, Substance Use, and Suicidal Ideation during the COVID-19 Pandemic—United States, June 24–30, 2020," *Morbidity and Mortality Weekly Report (MMWR)* 69, no. 32: 1049–57, https://www.cdc.gov/mmwr/volumes/69/wr/mm6932a1.htm?s_cid=mm6932a1_w.

5. Ben Wattenberg, "Divorce," from chapter four of *The First Measured Century*, PBS Program, https://www.pbs.org/fmc/book/4family6.htm.

6. Mark Banschick, "The High Failure Rate of Second and Third Marriages," *Psychology Today*, February 6, 2012, https://www.psychologytoday.com/us/blog/the -intelligent-divorce/201202/the-high-failure-rate-second-and-third-marriages.

CHAPTER 3: THE LIFE CONTINUUM SCALE

1. See 1 Samuel 31.

2. See Judges 16.

3. Ancient accounts of suicide are not limited to the Bible. A four-thousand-year-old Egyptian papyrus in the Berlin Museum gives an account of a man talking with his "ka" (soul) about suicide and his soul warning him against it.

4. The United States currently leads the world in murder-suicides. Further evidence of the entire scale shifting in one direction or the other is seen in the fact that the groups that commit suicide most frequently are also the groups that most often commit murder-suicides.

5. See Matthew 25:31-46 and Romans 2:14.

6. See Matthew 6:1.

7. Andrew Wu, Jing-Yu Wang, and Cun-Xian Jia, "Religion and Completed Suicide: A Meta-Analysis," *PLOS ONE*, June 25, 2015, https://journals.plos.org/plosone /article?id=10.1371/journal.pone.0131715.

8. Connie Svob et al., "Association of Parent and Offspring Religiosity with Offspring Suicide Ideation and Attempts," *JAMA Psychiatry* 75, no. 10 (2018): 1062–70, https://jamanetwork.com/journals/jamapsychiatry/fullarticle/2695329. It takes an immensely complicated subject and provides a framework for the rest of the book.

9. Herman M. van Praag, "The Role of Religion in Suicide Prevention," in Camilla Wasserman and Danuta Wasserman, *Oxford Textbook of Suicidology and Suicide Prevention* (Oxford: Oxford University Press, 2009), 7.

10. T. Dazzi et al., "Does Asking about Suicide and Related Behaviours Induce Suicidal Ideation? What Is the Evidence?" *Psychological Medicine* 44, no. 16 (December 2014): 3361–63, https://pubmed.ncbi.nlm.nih.gov/24998511/.

11. Jeremiah 29:11, NIV, emphasis added.

CHAPTER 4: MENTAL HEALTH 101

1. Most are familiar with the dreadful legacy of the Spanish Inquisition, the trial of Galileo, the Salem witch trials, and other persecutions of secular people by the organized church. Nothing can excuse these excesses. But they pale in comparison to secular movements that have thrown off God and persecute people of faith. The initial three centuries of Christian persecution by Rome, the persecutions of the church under the French Revolution as well as during Mao's Great Leap Forward, the Russian Revolution and Stalin's persecution of the church, as well as Fascist persecutions by Hitler, Mussolini, and others, illustrate how hundreds of millions have been slaughtered when God is left out of the equation.
2. See Matthew 15:1-20.
3. See Matthew 11:2-6; Luke 7:20-23.

CHAPTER 5: SUICIDE AND SATAN

1. See Matthew 12:30.
2. See, for example, John 8:12; 2 Corinthians 11:14; 1 John 1:5.
3. See Job 42:7.
4. See, for example, James 5:11.
5. See John 10:10; 1 Peter 5:8.
6. See John 12:6.
7. See Matthew 27:5; Acts 1:18.
8. See Acts 5:1-10.

CHAPTER 6: GOD AND SUICIDE

1. My paraphrase of Numbers 11:15.
2. See 1 Kings 19:15-16.
3. It is interesting to note that sophisticated Greeks and Romans had particular troubles with this story from the Hebrew Scriptures. They felt it was impossible for Jonah to be resurrected from within the belly of a whale. Yet if God can speak a universe into existence, what is so hard about resurrecting someone? Jesus said the Kingdom of Heaven was made up of children, and I've told this story to a number of them. I recall teaching in a park in Santa Barbara one afternoon with about twenty-five young people sitting on the ground in front of me. They ranged in age from first to sixth grade. Unlike older students who try to hide when they don't know something, these youngsters were filled with questions. But not one questioned God's ability to spit Jonah out of a whale. Of such is the Kingdom of Heaven. Moreover, Jesus specifically references the story of Jonah as prefiguring his own resurrection, thus affirming its accuracy. If Jesus believes it's true, that's proof enough for my little brain. If you would like to dig deeper into this story, please see J. Vernon McGee's thoughts on this subject: https://www.ttb.org/docs/default-source/booklets/jonah-dead-or-alive.pdf?sfvrsn=2.
4. What is the difference between "divers diseases" and "torments" referenced in this passage? I don't know. But I can tell you the difference between those possessed by devils and those who were lunatic. I believe that here "lunatic" represents those with epilepsy. In modern societies, epilepsy is present in about one percent of the

population. Someone you know has epilepsy. For most today, seizures are controlled by anti-seizure medicines. But sometimes, the seizures will "break through" the medications. One of the most common causes for this is that the person with epilepsy gets overly tired, the brain chemistry changes, and they become more susceptible to seizures as the seizure threshold is lowered. Keep in mind that in Jesus' time, no one had any treatment for seizures. Also in Jesus' time lighting was expensive. When the sun went down, people went to bed because it was dark. The only times that people could work or travel outside at night was during full moons (a harvest moon). During times when everyone could be up longer—i.e., during full moons—the rate of seizures increased. It is likely that they overworked and slept less during the full moon, and so their seizure threshold was likewise lowered. People seemed to get seizures because of the full moon (*luna* in Latin) and were thus called "lunatic."

CHAPTER 7: DRUGS AND ALCOHOL
1. See Genesis 9:18-27.
2. See Genesis 19:30-38.
3. For these two stories, see Exodus 32:1-6 and Leviticus 10:1-11.
4. See Esther 3:15.
5. See John 2:1-11.
6. My paraphrase of John 2:10.
7. See also Mark 4:41.
8. See Luke 7:34.
9. See Matthew 26:29.
10. See John 19:29-30.
11. Although no longer widely used, the efficacy of the mandrake is illustrated in books written in the era of doctors like A. J. Cronin and Sinclair Lewis, where it is used in preference to morphine to treat pain.
12. See Mark 15:23.
13. See, for example, Ephesians 5:18 and Titus 1:7.

CHAPTER 8: TALKING TO A LOVED ONE
1. See Exodus 23:5; Luke 10:25-37.
2. See Matthew 5:29-30.
3. See Deuteronomy 31:6; Matthew 28:20; Hebrews 13:5.
4. See Luke 19:1-10.
5. See Ezekiel 33:11.
6. See Matthew 6:25.

CHAPTER 9: PASTORS AND SUICIDE
1. See 2 Corinthians 11:24-25.
2. See Romans 8:38-39.
3. See Genesis 18:22-33; Exodus 32:11; Luke 23:34; Acts 7:60.
4. See John 5:22; Matthew 25:1-13; 13:42; Luke 16:19-31.
5. See, for example, Luke 13:10-17; 6:6-11; 4:24-29.

6. See James 3:1.
7. I've written a book about Sabbath (*24/6: A Prescription for a Healthier, Happier Life*, Tyndale, 2012) and worked with thousands of pastors on the specific challenges of Sabbath rhythms for clergy. Please see the many resources designed for both pastors and their congregations at SabbathLiving.org.

CHAPTER 10: THE CHURCH AND SUICIDE

1. There are several books written about how he dealt with depression and how he used the Bible and his faith to overcome it. If you want to learn more about Spurgeon and his battle with depression, I suggest starting with Zack Eswine's *Spurgeon's Sorrows*.
2. See Matthew 25:31-46, ESV.
3. Holly Hough et al., "Relationships between Sabbath Observance and Mental, Physical, and Spiritual Health in Clergy," *Pastoral Psychology* 68, no. 2 (2019): 171–93, https://divinity.duke.edu/sites/divinity.duke.edu/files/documents/chi /Hough_formatted.pdf.
4. See Revelation 11:18.
5. See Psalm 96 and 1 Chronicles 16:33.
6. See Matthew 10:29.
7. See Psalm 84:3.
8. See Proverbs 3:18.
9. *Reforesting Faith: What Trees Teach Us about the Nature of God and His Love for Us* (Colorado Springs: WaterBrook, 2019).
10. See Revelation 22:13-14.

THE HOPE ALWAYS TOOL KIT

1. This policy is adapted from "Creating a Church Suicide Prevention Policy," March 6, 2019, https://churchandmentalhealth.com/creating-a-church-suicide -prevention-policy/.
2. "Youth: How to Help," The National Suicide Prevention Lifeline, accessed October 21, 2020, https://suicidepreventionlifeline.org/help-yourself/youth/.
3. The direct link to these resources is https://www.psychiatry.org/psychiatrists /cultural-competency/engagement-opportunities/mental-health-and-faith -community-partnership.

About the Author

Matthew Sleeth, MD, a former emergency room physician and chief of the hospital medical staff, resigned from his position to teach, preach, and write about faith and health. Dr. Sleeth has spoken at more than one thousand churches, campuses, and events, including serving as a monthly guest preacher at the Washington National Cathedral. Recognized by *Newsweek* as one of the nation's most influential Christian leaders, Dr. Sleeth is the executive director of Blessed Earth and author of numerous articles and books. He lives in Lexington, Kentucky, with Nancy, his wife of forty years. Their grown children serve with their families in full-time parish ministry and as medical missionaries in Africa.

ALSO FROM TYNDALE HOUSE PUBLISHERS
AND DR. MATTHEW SLEETH . . .

24/6 AND THE 24/6
DVD EXPERIENCE!

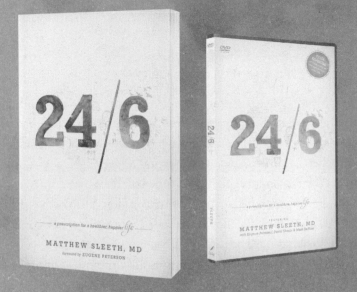

IN 24/6, DR. MATTHEW SLEETH DESCRIBES THE SYMPTOMS, clarifies the signs, diagnoses the illness, and lays out a simple plan for helping you live a healthier life. Matthew will help you transform your life not only physically but also emotionally, relationally, and spiritually simply by adopting the 24/6 lifestyle.

And once you've read the book, do the study! Join Dr. Matthew Sleeth in a four-session video study as he teaches you exactly how to live a healthier, more God-centered life in this digitally dazed, always-on world.

TYNDALE.COM   CP1664